D1039624

THE HONOR OF MY BROTHERS

. . . as for me, I do not wish to be held in high regard because of titles but because of deeds. Nor do I regard as an honor whatever I know to take away from the honor of my brothers. For my honor is the honor of the universal Church; my honor is the solid strength of my brothers. Then am I truly honored when the honor due to all and each is not denied them.

—Pope Gregory the Great,
Letter to Eulogius, July 598

UT UNUM SINT: STUDIES ON PAPAL PRIMACY

THE HONOR
OF MY
BROTHERS

A SHORT HISTORY
OF THE RELATION BETWEEN
THE POPE AND THE BISHOPS

WILLIAM HENN, O.F.M. CAP.

A Herder and Herder Book
The Crossroad Publishing Company
New York

The Crossroad Publishing Company
370 Lexington Avenue, New York, NY 10017

Copyright © 2000 by William Henn

All rights reserved. No part of this book may be reproduced, stored in a
retrieval system, or transmitted, in any form or by any means, electronic,
mechanical, photocopying, recording, or otherwise, without the written
permission of The Crossroad Publishing Company.

Printed in the United States of America

Library of Congress Cataloging-in-Publication Data

Henn, William.
   The honor of my brothers : a short history of the relation between the
Pope and the bishops / William Henn.
       p.   cm.
   Includes bibliographical references.
   ISBN 0-8245-1803-9 (alk. paper)
   1. Popes—Primacy—History. 2. Bishops—History. 3. Catholic
Church—Bishops—History. I. Title.
BX1805.H43 2000
262'.1—dc21
                                                        99-050939

1   2   3   4   5   6   7   8   9   10   04   03   02   01   00

Contents

Introduction 7

1. Church Order before the "Council of the 318 Fathers" 15

2. "Preeminent in Charity": Primacy in the Earliest Centuries 30

3. "Peter Has Spoken through Leo": The Era of the Great Ecumenical Councils 51

4. Gregory the Great Looks North: Entering the Middle Ages 84

5. *Libertas ecclesiae:* The Reform of Gregory VII 102

6. A House Divided: Schism and Conciliarism 117

7. The Struggle over Authority: Trent to Vatican I 129

8. Vatican II: Communion, Collegiality, and Primacy 143

Concluding Reflections 158

Index 164

5

Introduction

"From the Church of God
Sojourning in Rome"

These words appear at the beginning of Clement's letter to the Corinthians, one of the first Christian writings to come down to us after the New Testament. If the date ordinarily assigned to it is correct (around the year 96), then it probably was composed even earlier than the last books of the New Testament. The author begins with what seems to be an apology: "Because of our recent series of unexpected misfortunes and set-backs, my dear friends, we feel there has been some delay in turning our attention to the causes of dispute in your community" (*Letter to the Corinthians* 1).[1] Evidently the Corinthians would have had reason to expect even earlier a letter "from the Church of God sojourning in Rome."

Letters played a prominent role in the Christian community right from the start. How different the New Testament would be were one to imagine it without its letters, filled as they are with so many magnificent passages that have inspired Christians time and again over the centuries. In addition to their inspirational value, the letters reflect the life of the apostolic churches more directly than the other New Testament writings. One can read between the lines of the Gospel of John in order to draw out what must have been some of the

---

[1] The translation is taken from *Early Christian Writings: The Apostolic Fathers,* by Maxwell Staniforth (Middlesex: Penguin Books, 1987), 23. The "recent . . . misfortunes" of which Clement speaks are the persecution of Christians that took place in Rome under Domitian in 93; see ibid., 57 n. 2.

concerns of "the community of the beloved disciple," as Raymond Brown has so masterfully done. But the letters to the Corinthians, to the Galatians, or to Timothy and Titus all treat issues of the faith and order of the churches to whom they are addressed in a very direct and explicit way.

One characteristic of letters that has particular importance for the topic of this book is the obvious fact that, of their very nature, letters build bridges between people and communities located in different places. In the New Testament, Paul's letters put him in touch with the various local churches that had come into being through the positive reception of his proclamation of the gospel. Circular letters, such as the letter to the Galatians or the first letter of Peter, would have been common points of reference for those communities who shared them: "Peter, an apostle of Jesus Christ, to those who live as strangers scattered throughout Pontus, Galatia, Cappadocia, Asia and Bithynia; to those chosen according to the foreknowledge of God the Father, consecrated by the Spirit to a life of obedience to Jesus Christ and purification with his blood. Favor and peace be yours in abundance" (1 Pet. 1:1–2).

This practice by which persons and local communities would keep in touch with one another and thus maintain a communion that was broader than simply that of the local church continued in post–New Testament times. Almost all of the earliest noncanonical Christian writings, commonly grouped under the heading "the Apostolic Fathers," are letters. With time, the custom of exchanging letters between churches for the specific purpose of expressing communion with each other—for example, on the occasion of the election and consecration of a new bishop in a given city—became a very widespread and integral part of the life of the church.[2]

---

[2] A fascinating study of communion in the early church which shines some light on the role that letters played, especially as means by which Christians were able to join the local communities and the celebrations of the Eucharist in cities to which they traveled is Ludwig Hertling, *Com-*

Less than one hundred years after Jesus' death, a letter from Ignatius of Antioch contains what became an often quoted line: "Where the bishop is, there is the community; just as where Jesus Christ is, there is the catholic Church" (*Letter to the Smyrnaeans* 8). The unity of local churches within the larger "catholic" communion which embraces the whole body of Christ is the ultimate theological foundation for the relations that link the individual bishops to each other. This broader communion is also the foundation that provides the rationale for a ministry of primacy in service to the universal unity binding together all bishops and all local churches.

The fact that the letter is the precise literary form adopted by the earliest Christian writers, even those of the New Testament, helps to attenuate the first problem that anyone must face in seeking to provide a historical overview of the relation between the pope and the bishops. That problem is contained in the question: Where does the story begin? When one recalls the wide consensus among theologians and historians that the threefold ministry of bishop, presbyter, and deacon required some time to become the form of ministry universally characteristic of the local Christian communities, then it could seem anachronistic to speak of relations between bishops in the earliest decades of church history. Might it not be possible that, at least in the earliest decades, some communities may not have had a single bishop as leader of the community?[3] Moreover, the word "pope," deriving from a familiar Greek term for "father," was, for several hundred

---

munio: Church and Papacy in Early Christianity (Chicago: Loyola University Press, 1972).

[3] The International Theological Commission took up the problem of reconciling the historical development of ministry with the conviction that Jesus himself is the author of the essential ministerial structures of the church; see "Catholic Teaching on Apostolic Succession," in *International Theological Commission: Texts and Documents 1969–1985,* ed. M. J. Sharkey (San Francisco: Ignatius Press, 1989), 93–104.

years, a title commonly given to any bishop.[4] As late as the end of the sixth century, Pope Gregory the Great criticized the use of the word "ecumenical" or "universal" to qualify any one bishop for fear of detracting from the honor due them all.[5] Obviously, one must be careful in describing the relations "between the pope and the bishops" in these early centuries, lest one impose upon those times a conception that developed only later or that may only properly belong to a more recent stage of the life of the church. Joseph Ratzinger once wrote that only after the first ecumenical council of Nicaea, in 325, could the question of the relation between primacy and episcopacy be posed as one might pose it today.[6] Only when the ecumenical councils actually assembled a large number of bishops who could be seen as representing, at least in an approximate way, the episcopate as a whole, could the church begin to explore the parameters of the relation between the bishop of Rome, to whom even Ignatius of Antioch (d. 117) attributed a certain "primacy of love," and the body of bishops as a whole.

And yet the perplexities that derive from the evidence that ministry and the names used to describe it took shape over a long period of time should not blind us to the even more significant fact that, right from the start, the many local Christian communities had a sense of being part of one body, whose head is Jesus Christ. Right from the beginning, both

---

[4] So Y. Congar, "Titres donnés au pape," *Concilium* 108 (1975): 56–57.

[5] *Ad Eulogium episc. Alexandrinum,* epist. 30, lib. 8, in *Patrologiae cursus completus: Series latina,* ed. J. P. Migne, 221 vols. (Paris: Garnier-Migne, 1844–65), vol. 77, col. 933C. Hereafter this series will be referred to as Migne, *PL,* followed by the volume and column numbers. Quoted by Bishop Haynald at Vatican I; see J. D. Mansi, *Sacrorum conciliorum nova et amplissima collectio . . . ,* 53 vols. (Florence/Venice/Paris/Leipzig: H. Welter, 1759–1927), vol. 52, col. 666d. Hereafter this series will be referred to as Mansi, followed by the volume and column numbers.

[6] Joseph Ratzinger, *Das Neue Volk Gottes* (Düsseldorf: Patmos, 1969), 132.

within local churches and guiding them, were ministries that effectively served unity, both the internal unity of each individual community and the broader communion that united them with one another throughout the world. The letter is a very humble but powerful witness to this. In the early centuries, it is precisely the letter that provides the principal information about contacts between bishops, especially those involving the bishop of Rome. For the first several hundred years, the only literary works that survive from the bishops of Rome are letters. Only with Leo the Great (440–461) does one begin to see other writings, such as homilies. Yet this form has remained indispensable right up until the present, when letters addressed to individuals or groups and encyclicals addressed to the whole church continue to serve as a primary means by which the bishop of Rome carries out a ministry of promoting the catholic unity of the whole people of God.

Of course, the story of the relation between the pope and the bishops must draw upon many other literary resources as well. Even in the pre-Nicaean era, theological works by writers such as Irenaeus and Cyprian, or later histories of that period such as Eusebius, offer valuable information. To these should be added official documents, such as the canons of the early councils. As time goes on, the relevant documentation increases. It is probably no exaggeration to say that one would need an entire lifetime to work through all of the material relevant to the relationship between the primacy and the episcopacy.

Moreover, this material is not all of equal weight. The forgeries, such as the Pseudo-Isidorian Decretals, which insisted on papal authority to the detriment of the metropolitan archbishops, must obviously be given less importance than the genuine canons of councils such as Nicaea (325) or Sardica (343). And in the latter examples, the authority of a council such as Sardica should not be confused with that of Nicaea, which enjoys the dignity of being "ecumenical" or recognized as authoritative by all of the local churches. A number of bishops of Rome seem to have attributed Sardica's canons about the pope's authority as a court of appeal to Nicaea, which sometimes sparked no little resistance, as by the bishops of Carthage in the early fifth century. Finally, one needs to distinguish the teachings of individual theologians and ecclesiastical authors from the officially accepted doctrines about the relation between primacy and episcopacy. Individual writers backed diametrically opposed views. Some have affirmed that the bishops so depend on the pope that their authority derives entirely from him; others have insisted that the pope's primatial role is so conditioned by the authority of the local bishops that he cannot act outside of his own see of Rome apart from their agreement. The two Vatican councils (1869–1870 and 1962–1965), which offer the most extensive official teaching about the relation between the pope and the bishops, seem to avoid adopting the more exaggerated positions, either papalist or episcopalist.

A relatively short study of the history of the relation between the pope and the bishops cannot hope to be exhaustive. Many specific testimonies inevitably will be left out, some deliberately and others because of the human limitations of the author. Nevertheless, it does seem possible to give a short but substantially accurate description of this relation as it developed through the centuries.[7] Moreover, a brief yet

---

[7] One takes heart from the fact that the following short works do succeed in giving a reasonably credible overview of the periods of the papacy that they treat: Y. Congar, "La collegialità dell' episcopato e il primato del vescovo di Roma nella storia," in *Ministeri e comunione ecclesiale* (Bologna: Edizioni Dehoniane, 1973), 81–104; B. Tierney, "Pope and Bishops before Trent: An Historical Survey," in *The Papacy and the Church in the United States* (New York: Paulist Press, 1989), 11–23; G. Dejaifve, "Les douze apôtres et leur unité dans la tradition catholique," in *L'Épiscopat et l'Église universelle* (Paris: Cerf, 1962), 760–78; and K. Schatz, *Papal Primacy: From Its Origins to the Present* (Collegeville, Minn.: Liturgical Press, 1996). In addition to these, the great histories of ecclesiology by Yves Congar (*Die Lehre von der Kirche: Von Augustinus*

sound historical overview is indispensable to any dialogue about the forms of exercising the primacy in today's changed ecumenical situation, such as the dialogue to which Pope John Paul II courageously invited other church leaders and their theologians in *Ut unum sint* §§95–96. History is one of the greatest of teachers, helping the student to distinguish what is essential from what is not. But history is also vulnerable to ideological manipulation, as the Faith and Order Commission so well pointed out in its recent study document *In Earthen Vessels: Toward an Ecumenical Hermeneutics.*[8] I confess from the outset my bias as a Catholic theologian who looks at history with the eyes of faith, searching for what God may be about in the human story of the church. This has led me to be attentive to what is positive in the story, hopefully without turning a blind eye to what is negative. My hope is that the following analysis is true and that the insights gathered from this historical investigation can contribute to the ongoing dialogue about the relation between the papacy and the episcopacy that will bear fruit in the future.

---

bis zum Abendländischen Schisma and *Vom Abendländischen Schisma bis zur Gegenwart,* Band III, 3c and 3d of *Handbuch der Dogmengeschichte* (Freiburg/BaselVienna: Herder, 1971); hereafter *HDG* III, 3c or 3d) and by Angel Antón (*El misterio de la Iglesia,* I and II [Madrid/Toledo: BAC, 1986, 1987]).

[8]Geneva: WCC Publications, 1998.

CHAPTER 1

Church Order before the "Council of the 318 Fathers"

A Deserted and Untrodden Road

Eusebius, bishop of Caesarea, the principal see of the ecclesiastical province that included Jerusalem, wrote the final version of his *Ecclesiastical History* sometime after the year 323, when Constantine became the sole ruler of the Roman Empire. His book begins with a statement of purpose; the author intends . . .

> to hand down a written account of the successions of the holy Apostles as well as of the times extending from our Saviour to ourselves; the number and nature of the events which are said to have been treated in ecclesiastical history; the number of those who were her illustrious guides and leaders in especially prominent dioceses; the number of those who in each generation by word of mouth or by writings served as ambassadors of the word of God; the names, the number, and the times of those who out of a desire for innovation launched into an extremity of error and proclaimed themselves the introducers of knowledge falsely so called, mercilessly ravaging the flock of Christ like ravening wolves; and besides this what straightway befell the entire Jewish race as the result of its plot against our Saviour; furthermore, the number, and times of the war waged by the Gentiles against the divine Word; and the character of those who on various occasions have passed through the contest of blood and tortures on His behalf; and, in addition to this, the martyrdoms

of our own times and with them all the gracious and kindly succor of our Saviour.[1]

Quite an ambitious undertaking! Eusebius acknowledges that he is traveling "a deserted and untrodden road," no one having yet written a narrative of this scope about the church. He asks for his readers' indulgence, acknowledging that, for some periods, he was "unable to discover even the bare tracks of those who traveled the same path before us." How well did he succeed?

Reactions to Eusebius have been mixed. Many commentators express appreciation for the fact that his history contains an abundance of information that otherwise would have been forever lost. Some even think of him as a reasonably reliable historian.[2] Others point out what appear to be the biases that color his narrative. One of the more lively debates of twentieth-century patristic scholarship was sparked by Walter Bauer's *Orthodoxy and Heresy in Earliest Christianity*, which begins with a thorough critique of Eusebius's "ideological" reading of the history of the ancient church.[3] According to Bauer, Eusebius naively presupposes that the church enjoyed a state of doctrinal purity at the beginning, only later to be corrupted by heretical innovations. The history of doctrine must be written the other way around, he argues. What eventually came to be known as "orthodoxy" only gradually emerged.

---

[1] Eusebius Pamphili, *Ecclesiastical History*, books 1–5, trans. Roy J. Deferrari, The Fathers of the Church 19 (Washington, D.C.: Catholic University of America Press, 1953), 35–36.

[2] So Patrick Hamell, *Handbook of Patrology* (Staten Island, N.Y.: Alba House, 1968), 94–95. Johannes Quasten is more cautious but also quite positive: "He makes no effort at a complete or well-balanced account, much less does he attempt an orderly and reasoned exposition of the spread and growth of Christianity. His work represents an extremely rich collection of historical facts, documents and excerpts from a multitude of writings of the early Church" (*Patrology* [Westminster: Newman Press, 1960], 3:314).

[3] W. Bauer, *Orthodoxy and Heresy in Earliest Christianity* (Philadelphia: Fortress Press, 1971; orig. 1934).

Not all would agree with Bauer's reading of history either.[4] At least one positive outcome of disagreements about the reliability of Eusebius is that they encourage modesty in drawing conclusions about the period covered by his *Ecclesiastical History*. When compared with later centuries, the resources that tell of this earliest period are relatively sparse and open to various interpretations. This is especially true with regard to the precise topic of the present study: the relation between the bishop of Rome and the other bishops.

Eusebius attended the council that the emperor Constantine convoked at Nicaea in 325 to deal with the doctrinal divisions caused by the teachings of Arius. One dramatic feature of this first ecumenical council, held within memory of the last general persecution of Christians under Diocletian, was the presence of many bishops who bore the scars of having been tortured for their faith. At Nicaea one could see the church coming out from hiding, after centuries of intermittent persecution. It was reported that 318 bishops attended this first ecumenical council. This detail inspired some patristic writers to liken these council fathers to the 318 members of the household of Abram, "our father in faith" (Rom. 4:11–12), who triumphed by the sword over the kidnappers of Abram's kinsman Lot in Gen. 14:13–16. Nicaea was a triumph for faith in Jesus Christ. In addition, it ushered in a new era of relations between church leaders and, in particular, between the bishop of Rome and the leaders of other local churches.

But if one wishes to go back before Nicaea, before the

---

[4] Challenging many of the details of the Bauer thesis is Thomas A. Robinson, *The Bauer Thesis Examined: The Geography of Heresy in the Early Church* (Lewiston: Edwin Mellen, 1988). I have tried to show that, even in the New Testament, the variety evident when comparing the particular theological slant of the individual authors is held together by a fundamental unity in faith, a unity fostered and maintained by various factors constitutive of the life of the community (see W. Henn, *One Faith: Biblical and Patristic Contributions Toward Understanding Unity in Faith* [Mahwah, N.J.: Paulist Press, 1995], 60–85).

"Council of the 318," can one find data that illuminate the relation between the bishop of Rome and the other bishops? Can one speak of a "primacy" before Nicaea? And this question leads inexorably to another. "Primacy" is a category that singles out one of a particular class as somehow "first" in relation to the others of the same group. Thus it presupposes both the existence of such a group and some pattern by which its members relate to each other. The present chapter must examine this presupposition of a ministry of primacy among bishops by seeking to uncover how bishops related to one another before Nicaea. On this foundation, chapter 2 will then examine the evidence for primacy in the earliest three centuries.

"Follow your bishop, every one of you,
as obediently as Jesus Christ followed the Father"
(Ignatius of Antioch, To the Smyrnaeans 8)

The New Testament does not provide a clear and unambiguous picture of the structure of the earliest Christian communities. To be sure, there are numerous indications of a variety of ministries and roles in service to the community right from the start.[5] Acts 1:15–26 presents Peter leading the nascent community in discerning whom God had chosen "to take the place in this ministry and apostleship from which Judas turned aside." Acts 6:1–6 shows the Twelve guiding the community to resolve the problem that arose when the Hellenist widows were being neglected in the daily distribution of food; seven men were chosen by the community and set before the apostles, who prayed and laid hands upon

---

[5] G. O'Collins argues that only biased exegesis could construe the New Testament witness as evidence in support of a radically unstructured community ("Did Apostolic Continuity Ever Start? Origins of Apostolic Continuity in the New Testament," *Louvain Studies* 21 [1996]: 138–52). A recent sketch of the biblical roots of ministerial structures is offered by John F. O'Grady, *Disciples and Leaders: The Origins of Christian Ministry in the New Testament* (Mahwah, N.J.: Paulist Press, 1991).

them. Toward the end of the account of their first great missionary journey (Acts 13–14), Paul and Barnabas are said to have returned to the various new communities of believers that they had established: "And when they appointed elders (*presbyteroi*) for them in every church, with prayer and fasting, they committed them to the Lord in whom they believed" (Acts 14:23). In the "council" that met in Jerusalem to resolve the question of the applicability of the Jewish law to Gentile converts, "the apostles and the elders" figure prominently (Acts 15:4, 6, 22, 23) within the whole assembly (Acts 15:12, 22). When Paul says good-bye to his beloved church at Ephesus, he speaks with the elders (Acts 20:17), who are also referred to as overseers or bishops (*episkopoi* [Acts 20:28]).

Such evidence is not only proper to the book of Acts, whose theme is to recount the birth and early growth of the Christian community. The entire New Testament contains references to various ministries and roles of leadership, from the accounts of the call and mission of the disciples in the Synoptic Gospels (Matt. 10:1–42; 28:16–20; Mark 3:13–19; 16:15–20; Luke 5:1–11; 6:12–16) to the lists of ministries in the letters of Paul: "apostles, prophets, teachers, miracle workers, healers, assistants, administrators and those who speak in tongues" (1 Cor. 12:28; cf. Rom. 12:6–8; Eph. 4:11). The pastoral letters describe the qualities needed in bishops (1 Tim. 3:1–11; Titus 1:7–9), presbyters (Titus 1:5–6), and deacons (1 Tim. 3:12–13). The many individual references that constitute the "Petrine trajectory" find their high point in three dialogues in which Jesus himself singles Peter out from the rest of the disciples and assigns to him a particular task or function (Matt. 16:17–19; Luke 22:31–32; John 21:15–19).[6] Notwithstanding all of this, the New Tes-

---

6 The New Testament work on Peter has been voluminous. Some recent contributions are S. Cipriani et al., "Contributi Petriani," *Miscellanea Francescana* 74 (1974) 273–432; A. Brandenburg and H. J. Urban, eds., *Petrus und Papst: Evangelium, Einheit der Kirche, Papstdienst* (Münster:

tament does not take up the specific task of describing in detail the church order of any particular local community. Indeed, even those texts that use ministerial terms such as "presbyter" or "bishop-overseer," seem to use them interchangeably, making it unclear whether these ministries are distinct or, if so, what the precise difference between them may be.[7]

Three Bishops: Ignatius, Clement, and Irenaeus

This New Testament ambiguity stands in sharp contrast to the vision of church order offered by Ignatius of Antioch's seven letters, all written as he was heading toward Rome to be devoured by wild beasts during the reign of the emperor Trajan (98–117). For Ignatius, the unity of a local community around its bishop is willed by Christ himself. Its members should be "at one with their bishop—and with their clergy [presbyters] and deacons too, whose appointment with him is approved by Jesus Christ and confirmed and ratified, according to His will, by His Holy Spirit."[8] Ignatius sees the ministerial structure of the church as intimately related to the Eucharist. Just as there is one body and blood

---

Aschendorff, 1976); R. Pesch, *Simon-Petrus: Geschichte und geschichtliche Bedeutung des ersten Jüngers Jesu Christi* (Stuttgart: Hiersemann, 1980), and, having a special credibility because of its ecumenical origin, Raymond E. Brown, Karl P. Donfried, John Reumann, eds., *Peter in the New Testament* (Minneapolis: Augsburg, 1973), from which I have borrowed the expression "Petrine trajectory."

[7] Raymond E. Brown, *Priest and Bishop* (New York: Paulist Press, 1970), 34–40.

[8] From the opening greeting of *The Epistle to the Philadelphians*, trans. M. Staniforth, in *Early Christian Writings* (Middlesex: Penguin Books, 1987), 111. Staniforth translates the word *presbyteroi* with the word "clergy," which obscures the fact that Ignatius wishes to single out with this term a specific group within the "clergy," that is, the presbyters. Hereafter, in following this translation I will substitute the word "presbyters" for "clergy." References to Ignatius's letters will be made in the text, simply giving the community to which they were written and paragraph number.

of the one savior Jesus Christ, so too the Christian community must be one, a unity that is maintained when all remain united under the guidance of their appointed ministers.

> Make certain, therefore, that you all observe one common Eucharist; for there is but one Body of our Lord Jesus Christ, and but one cup of union with His Blood, and one single altar of sacrifice—even as also there is but one bishop, with his presbyters and my own fellow servitors the deacons. This will ensure that all your doings are in full accord with the will of God. (*Philadelphians* 4)

In another letter, he remarks that "the sole Eucharist you should consider valid is one that is celebrated by the bishop himself, or by some person authorized by him," adding a sentence that became famous as the first instance that the adjective "catholic" was used to describe the Christian community: "Where the bishop is to be seen, there let all his people be, just as wherever Jesus Christ is present, we have the catholic Church" (*Smyrnaeans* 8).[9]

Ignatius uses the simile of musical harmony to describe the unity of the church when the bishop, the presbyters, and the people are all of one in faith.

> That is why it is proper for your conduct and your practices to correspond closely with the mind of the bishop. And this, indeed, they are doing; your justly respected presbyters, who are a credit to God, are attuned to their bishop like the strings of a harp, and the result is a hymn of praise to Jesus Christ from minds that are in unison, and affections that are in harmony. Pray, then, come and join this choir, every one of you;

---

[9] The precise meaning of the word "catholic" here has been an object of discussion. Is it primarily quantitative in meaning, so that the first part of the sentence which mentions the bishop refers to the local church, while the second half which mentions Jesus refers to the church universal? Or does "catholic" have the nuance of authenticity, completeness, and, in that sense, of doctrinal integrity and even orthodoxy? Probably both meanings are to be understood as part of Ignatius's intention here. See the opening chapters of W. Beinert, *Um das dritte Kirchenattribut: Die Katholizität der Kirche* (Essen: Ludgerus-Verlag H. Wingen, 1964).

let there be a whole symphony of minds in concert; take the tone all together from God, and sing aloud to the Father with one voice through Jesus Christ. . . . (*Ephesians* 4)

So important is this Christ-willed ecclesial order for the identity of the Christian community that Ignatius does not recognize as "church" any gathering of Christians that is outside of such a communal structure.

Equally, it is for the rest of you to hold the deacons in as great respect as Jesus Christ; just as you should look on the bishop as a type of the Father, and the presbyters as the Apostolic circle forming His council; for without these three orders no church has any right to the name. (*Trallians* 3; see also *Magnesians* 6)

Nothing should be undertaken within the community apart from the collaboration of its ordained ministers (see *Magnesians* 7; *Trallians* 2, 7).

In light of the less forceful biblical testimony about ecclesial structure, one is led inevitably to ask how it would have been possible, within the short space of time separating the New Testament authors from Ignatius, for the order of the Christian community to have become as clearly differentiated and well established as his letters would seem to suggest. Such a question has led some even to postpone the composition of at least some of the letters until several decades after their traditional dating (ca. 115). One thing seems sure: they prove that at least an early form of the threefold ministry of presbyters and deacons under the leadership of a single bishop was functioning in Ephesus, Magnesia, Tralles, Philadelphia, and Smyrna (the letters to Polycarp and to Rome do not speak of church order) at a relatively early time. Moreover, they clearly express Ignatius's view that such ministry either has been or should be adopted in every local church.[10] He champions this form of

---

[10] This is the view of James McCue, "The Roman Primacy in the Patristic Era: I, The Beginnings Through Nicea," in *Papal Primacy and the*

church order not only because he believes it is willed by Christ but also because it fosters unity within the local churches which are threatened by divisions.[11]

To Ignatius's testimony about ministry in these earliest decades should be added that of Clement of Rome's letter to the Corinthians, usually dated a bit earlier at around the year 96. Clement lacks Ignatius's clear-cut differentiation between the ministries of bishop, presbyter, and deacon. But what he does offer is the first post–New Testament expression of the doctrine of apostolic succession.

> Now, the Gospel was given to the Apostles for us by the Lord Jesus Christ; and Jesus the Christ was sent from God. That is to say, Christ received His commission from God, and the Apostles theirs from Christ. The order of these two events was in accordance with the will of God. So thereafter, when the Apostles had been given their instructions, and all their doubts had been set at rest by the resurrection of our Lord Jesus Christ from the dead, they set out in the full assurance of the Holy Spirit to proclaim the coming of God's kingdom. And as they went through the territories and townships preaching, they appointed their first converts—after testing them by the Spirit—to be bishops and deacons for the believers of the future. (*First Letter to the Corinthians* 42).[12]

Here the accent is not so much on the precise form of ministry as on its succession and its ability to be traced back to

---

Universal Church, ed. P. Empie and T. Austin Murphy (Minneapolis: Augsburg, 1974), 49–50.

[11] Robert Eno argues that Ignatius's "strong statements functioned within a sort of campaign to promote what he thought the churches needed, namely, the prestige and authority of a single leader in the local community, such as Polycarp in Smyrna. Like the author of the Pastoral Epistles, Ignatius feared the disintegration of the local community because of Docetists and Judaizers, if there were not a strong leader who could command obedience, in whom the identity of the Church could be anchored and around whom the faithful could rally" (*The Rise of the Papacy* [Wilmington, Del.: Michael Glazier, 1990], 23).

[12] From Staniforth and Louth, *Early Christian Writings*, 45.

the design of God. God sends Christ, who chooses the apostles, who in turn, with the assurance and discernment bestowed by the Holy Spirit, select bishops and deacons to lead the future communities.

Finally, these two dimensions of ministerial leadership are recognized as being intimately interrelated by Irenaeus of Lyon, when he writes his major work *Against the Heresies* around the year 180. According to Irenaeus, the bulwark of the church's defense against the divisive doctrines of the heretics is the vigilant ministry of the bishops, who succeed to one another in guiding the churches founded originally by the apostles. The ministry of bishops within the apostolic succession assures the doctrinal apostolicity of the church: what is believed in those churches *is* the apostolic faith. Teachings that contradict what is publicly taught in such apostolic churches is heretical. Irenaeus indicates that many churches had conserved lists of their bishops, a point that indicates just how important this succession was considered in his day. For his own part, he provides the list of the succession of bishops from that church whose prestige is particularly great because it rests on the ultimate witness (*martyria*) of the great apostles Peter and Paul, the church of Rome (*Against the Heresies* 3.3.2–3). Later Eusebius informs us that the historian Hegesippus had also compiled a list of the bishops of Rome (*Ecclesiastical History* 4.22).

By the year 200, no local church about which we have any information, with the possible exception of Alexandria, was without the structure described by Ignatius of Antioch. Each was guided by an individual bishop, along with his assisting presbyters and deacons.[13] Does the fact that this structure seems to have required the passage of some time before it took its definitive shape and spread to all the local churches throughout the world create a problem for the doctrine that

---

[13] See F. A. Sullivan, "Biblical and Historical Basis for the Teaching Authority of Bishops," in *Magisterium: Teaching Authority in the Catholic Church* (Mahwah, N.J.: Paulist Press, 1983), 35–44, especially 43.

Jesus himself established the essential ministerial structures of the church? Most Catholic theologians would think not. The conviction that God intended to furnish the church with some specific ministerial structures and that the foundation of such ministries is therefore "of divine law" (*iure divino*) need not exclude the gradual emergence of those structures, under the guidance of the Holy Spirit, within the community founded by Jesus.[14]

Cyprian: "The Bishop Is in the Church"

A good indication of how important the episcopal ministry was considered for the church can be found in the letters of Cyprian of Carthage, written between 249 and his martyrdom in 258. Writing to Florentius in 254, Cyprian pens some of the most often quoted words from the patristic period about the episcopacy: "the bishop is in the Church and the Church is in the bishop and, if there is anyone who is not with the bishop, he is not in the Church" (*Letter 66* 8).[15] Interestingly enough, this statement appears as a com-

---

[14] See the International Theological Commission, "Apostolic Succession" (see introduction, n. 3), perhaps more accessible in *Origins* 4 (1974): 193–200. The commission noted that much New Testament material supports the affirmation that Jesus himself stands at the origin of Christian ministry. However, on its own, historical research cannot prove that the developments leading to the episcopal ministry as described by Ignatius of Antioch were the only logical developments that could possibly flow from what the New Testament says about ministry. Only in faith can one discern the guidance of the Holy Spirit in a particular historical development. This being so, the fact that the bishop-presbyter-deacon structure became the universally adopted form of local church leadership only over an extended period of time in no way leads to the conclusion that this structure is not established by God or *de iure divino*. Eno seems to believe that historical development excludes divine institution (*Rise of the Papacy*, 19). Sullivan is more convincing when he argues that the two are compatible (*Magisterium*, 35–44).

[15] In *Saint Cyprian: Letters (1–81)*, trans. Sr. R. B. Donna, The Fathers of the Church 51 (Washington, D.C.: Catholic University of America Press,

ment about the profession of faith made by Peter in John 6:68–70: "Lord, to whom shall we go? You have the words of everlasting life; and we have believed and have come to know that you are the Holy One of God." Peter's world led Cyprian to think not so much about any one bishop, such as the bishop in the city where Peter died, but rather about all bishops. The profession of faith made by Peter must be made by every one of them. "There speaks Peter, upon whom the Church had been built, teaching in the name of the Church and showing that . . . the people united to their bishop and the flock clinging to their shepherd are the Church" (*Letter 66* 8).

In another passage, Cyprian ties together the episcopacy with what is perhaps the most famous Petrine text:

> Our Lord, whose precepts we ought to fear and to keep, assigning the honor of the bishop and the plan for His Church, speaks in the Gospel and says to Peter: I say to thee that thou art Peter, and upon this rock I will build my Church. . . . Thus through the changes of times and successions, the ordination of bishops and the organization of the Church run through so that the Church is established upon the bishops and every action of the Church is governed through these same prelates. (*Letter 33* 1)

These passages show that the title "successor to Peter" would have been understood by Cyprian as applying primarily to bishops. It is only about a hundred years later, when the primacy of the bishop of Rome becomes a more explicit topic of interest, that the popes begin to speak about succession to Peter as the principal biblical support for the unique primatial ministry that they exercised in service to the unity of the community as a whole. But obviously such a use of Petrine texts is not their only legitimate use. Indeed, in one of the earliest commentaries on Matt. 16:17–19, Origen interprets Peter's profession and Christ's response as referring neither

---

1964), 229. Hereafter, this translation will be used, giving within parentheses in the text the numbers of the letter and paragraph being cited.

to the primatial ministry of the bishop of Rome nor to the episcopal ministry of all bishops but rather to the faith of each and every individual believer.[16]

Cyprian thus understands the bishop as the foundation of each local church, in light of Jesus' words that he would found his church upon Peter and upon his profession of faith. This leads Cyprian to conclude that the cause of all heretical divisions is a departure from unity with the faith of the local bishop. "Nor from elsewhere have heresies sprung up nor have schisms been born than from this, that there is no obedience to the bishop of God . . ." (Cyprian to the bishop of Rome Cornelius, *Letter 59 5*; see also *Letter 66 5*). What holds the "catholic" church around the world together is precisely the unity of faith and love between bishops: "the Church which is one, Catholic, is not divided nor rent, but is certainly united and joined, in turn, by the solder of the bishops adhering to one another" (*Letter 66 8*).

Two points about Cyprian's vision of church order call for a further comment. First of all, the emphasis on the foundational necessity of the episcopacy seems to harmonize with what was proposed by Ignatius over a hundred years earlier. Why did these writers give this ministry such importance? Have they not perhaps exaggerated the role of the bishop, in such a way as to diminish everyone else in the Christian community? In one of his earlier essays, Joseph Ratzinger offered a plausible explanation of what he called the "massive theology of the episcopacy in Ignatius of Antioch [and] Cyprian of Carthage" by pointing to the public nature and "relative non-spontaneity" of the church.[17] The grace-assisted decision of faith by which one becomes part of the Christian

---

[16] See Eno, *Rise of the Papacy*, 42–43; Roland Minnerath, "La position de l'église de Rome aux trois premiers siècles," in *Il primato del Vescovo di Roma nel Primo Millennio* (Vatican City: Libreria Editrice Vaticana, 1991), 168; and especially McCue, "Roman Primacy in the Patristic Era: I, The Beginnings Through Nicea," 61.

[17] Joseph Ratzinger, "Primat und Episkopat," in *Das neue Volk Gottes* (Düsseldorf: Patmos, 1969), 122–23.

community is made freely and, in that sense spontaneously. But once within the community, determining with whom one celebrates the Eucharist is not a spontaneous decision. All of those who are believers in a particular place belong to the church, which is a public and stable community. One cannot choose to change the face of this community. This public nature of the church is essential to its unity as the people of God. The church is not a collection of private groups made up of individuals who at any given moment happen to decide to associate with each other. The idea that there be only one bishop in a local church, already present in Ignatius and included in the canons of the first ecumenical council in 325, follows from the conviction that the church is an indivisible, public community; it preserves the church from being suffocated by a myriad of private groups.

Second, how are these internally united local churches maintained in communion with one another? Cyril Vogel listed seven distinct means by which the supralocal communion of the church was maintained from the third through the fifth centuries.[18] One of these means—interventions by the Roman emperors such as the convocation of ecumenical councils—only occurred after the period we are considering in the present chapter. The same could also be said for another of Vogel's means: the collection and divulging of canons governing ecclesial discipline, the evidence for which is stronger at a later period. But the other five means were not only in use but, in varying degrees, indispensable to "catholic" unity even during this earliest period. They are (1) the presence of several bishops at every episcopal ordination, (2) the need for all bishops to honor the excommunications issued by any one of them, (3) the celebration of synods or councils to deal with questions affecting a broader

---

[18] C. Vogel, "Unité de l'Église et pluralité des formes historiques d'organisation ecclésiastique du IIIe au Ve siècle," in *L'Épiscopat et l'Église universelle*, ed. Y. Congar and B. D. Dupuy, Unam Sanctam 39 (Paris: Cerf, 1962), 591–636.

area than that of the local church, (4) the exchange of letters between bishops for various purposes (to notify others of the consecration of a new bishop, to ask hospitality for travelers, to seek advice or agreement on doctrinal issues, and to correct one another) and, finally, (5) interventions in the affairs of smaller churches by the bishops of more prominent sees, especially by the bishop of Rome.[19] These various means of maintaining supralocal unity obviously imply substantial contact between the bishops, as the leaders of the local churches. These leaders were not closed in upon their own communities; indeed, they could not be good leaders of the local community without keeping an eye open to relations with and concern for the other churches. In fact, every bishop of whom we have any knowledge during the second century—Clement, Anicetus, and Victor of Rome, Ignatius of Antioch, Polycarp of Smyrna, Dennis of Corinth, and Irenaeus of Lyon, to mention the most well known of them—all appear on the stage of history as leaders who not only shepherded their local communities but were actively engaged in promoting the broader well-being of the church as a whole.[20]

With the topic of relations between bishops, we finally arrive at the proper context for considering the exercise of "primacy" during this first period before the council of the 318 fathers. In its most fundamental sense, primacy refers to the exercise of a unique leadership role and authority by one bishop either within a particular area or within the college of all bishops taken together as a whole. Was there such a primatial exercise of authority, especially on the part of the bishop of Rome, in the first three centuries?

---

[19] Any one of these means of communion could easily provide sufficient material for a whole chapter or book. A short work that touches on most of these means of communion and which, furthermore, relates them to the primacy is Hertling, *Communio: Church and Papacy in Early Christianity* (see introduction, n. 2).

[20] See Minnerath, "La position de l'église de Rome aux trois premiers siècles," 150.

CHAPTER 2

"Preeminent in Charity":
Primacy in the Earliest Centuries

The letter of Clement to the Corinthians has sometimes been considered the first intervention by a bishop of Rome in the affairs of another local church. The church at Corinth was troubled by the fact that some of its members were rejecting the leadership of the community's ordained ministers (see paragraphs 3, 44–47). Clement urges humble submission to the clergy because their place within the community derives ultimately from God and from the mission that Christ entrusted to the apostles. As an exhortation correcting a problem in a community other than his own, the letter might be seen as a very early example (ca. 96) of the exercise of primacy by the bishop of Rome.[1]

Various problems were raised with this interpretation. First of all, the letter itself does not explicitly mention an individual named Clement. This attribution is owed to later writers, such as Irenaeus (*Against the Heresies* 3.3.3) and Eusebius (*Ecclesiastical History* 3.16). In addition, some have raised questions about whether Rome, at the time of the writing of the letter, had yet adopted the ecclesial structure

---

[1] Raymond E. Brown states that such an interpretation comes from "an older generation of catholic scholars" and has been abandoned since the 1930s (in R. Brown and J. Meier, *Antioch and Rome* [New York: Paulist Press, 1982], 162). See J. Fuellenbach, *Ecclesiastical Office and the Primacy of Rome: An Evaluation of Recent Theological Discussion of First Clement* (Washington, D.C.: Catholic University of America Press, 1980), for an overview of the range of views concerning Clement's letter and the primacy.

of having only one bishop (monepiscopacy). Most of all, the evidence that the exercise of primacy by the bishop of Rome developed over an extended period of time advised caution, lest one anachronistically misconstrue Clement's letter as the kind of primatial intervention that appeared only much later.[2]

All that being granted, this text nevertheless demonstrates the concern of the Roman church for the Christian community in Corinth during a moment of crisis. The Roman community felt entitled to intervene, apparently in response to a request by the Corinthians themselves. Was this due to the fact that Corinth was little more than a Roman colony at the time?[3] Or was it due to the fact that Corinth and Rome felt a unique bond because they both enjoyed a special connection with the two great apostles Peter and Paul (cf. the "Peter faction" of 1 Cor. 1:12)? Or was it simply an example of the normal concern that any local church might have for another? It is difficult to answer these questions with certainty. But we can begin to grasp the importance given to Clement's letter when we read a letter from Dionysius, bishop of Corinth, written some seventy years later to the Roman bishop Soter (166–175), stating that Clement's letter was still being read in his community on the Lord's Day (Eusebius, *Ecclesiastical History* 4.23). In another place, Eusebius adds that it was "used in public assembly in many

---

[2] Monepiscopacy and apostolic succession in relation to papal primacy are discussed by James McCue, "The Roman Primacy in the Patristic Era: I, The Beginnings Through Nicea," in *Papal Primacy and the Universal Church,* ed. P. Empie and T. Austin Murphy (Minneapolis: Augsburg, 1974), 44–72. The evidence concerning a single bishop in the city Rome is reviewed by Robert Eno (*The Rise of the Papacy* [Wilmington, Del.: Michael Glazier, 1990], 26–29) and Raymond Brown (*Antioch and Rome,* 162–64). None of these Catholic authors would see the historical development of the ministry of the bishop of Rome as constituting an insuperable problem for the official Catholic teaching about papal primacy.

[3] On this "colonial" status, see H. Marot, "Unité de l'Église et diversité géographique aux premiers siècles," in *L'Épiscopat et l'Église universelle,* ed. Y. Congar and B. D. Dupuy, Unam Sanctam 39 (Paris: Cerf, 1962), 577.

churches both in olden days and in our own time," thus
more than two hundred years after it was written (ibid.,
3.16)!

The Noble Witness of Peter and Paul

One further detail may ultimately provide the most important contribution of Clement's letter to any investigation of
the primacy. Methodist professor William R. Farmer argues
that the references in paragraph 5 to the example of patient
endurance unto death of Peter and Paul, "the noble figures
of our own generation," hint at the special role that the
church of Rome now is called to play because of its relation
to those two apostles.

> Out of deference to the church in Corinth which also
> regarded itself as having been founded by Peter and Paul,
> Clement of Rome makes no explicit reference to the place
> where these two apostles both rendered their "obedience
> unto death." But the whole procedure, where the church in
> Rome is exercising a responsibility to intervene in the inter-
> nal affairs of the church in Corinth, presupposes that some
> enormous transformation in the relationship between the
> churches in these two Roman cities has taken place. That one
> is in Rome and the other is in a colony of Rome simply can-
> not be the explanation for this astounding development in
> church polity. . . . The most satisfactory explanation for the
> facts as we know them is that the church in Rome is exercis-
> ing an authority which proceeds from its vocation to live out
> of the united witness of these two "good" apostles (as
> Clement gently puts it), and to help other churches to do the
> same.[4]

This connection with the apostles Peter and Paul also
appears as the most significant detail in the next two writings which have some relevance for the question of primacy:
Ignatius of Antioch's *Epistle to the Romans* and Irenaeus of

---

[4] In William R. Farmer and Roch Kereszty, O.Carm., *Peter & Paul in
the Church of Rome* (New York: Paulist Press, 1990), 21.

Lyon's *Adversus Haereses*. Ignatius begs the Romans not to try to save him from martyrdom and even to pray that he "may be made a worthy sacrifice to God," adding "however, I am not issuing orders to you, as though I were a Peter or a Paul" (*Romans* 4). This seems to be clear evidence already from the time of Ignatius that Peter and Paul had ministered in Rome. Moreover, while Ignatius's letters to the other churches contain various exhortations and admonitions, the one to Rome seems much more laudatory. It is addressed to "the church holding chief place in the territories of the district of Rome—worthy of God, worthy of honour, blessing, praise, and success; worthy too in holiness, foremost in love, observing the law of Christ, and bearing the Father's Name."

Two phrases from this greeting should be pointed out. First of all, the phrase "holding chief place in the territories . . . of Rome" suggests some kind of regional grouping of churches, perhaps the beginnings of that "metropolitan" system which tied a number of local churches to a principal see, parallel to some of the subdivisions within the Roman Empire. The next evidence of the existence of such regional groupings will appear in the synods held toward the end of the second century to address the question of the celebration of Easter (see Eusebius, *Ecclesiastical History* 5.23–24). Here Ignatius seems to be recognizing Rome as the principal church of its ecclesiastical region.

Second, the expression "foremost in love" or, more literally, "presiding in love" has received various interpretations, including, in our own day, the view that it represents a kind of presidency of the churches sharply in contrast to the "primacy of jurisdiction" defined at Vatican I. What did it mean to Ignatius? Johannes Quasten has interpreted the word "love" (*agapē*) as referring to the communion that unites the whole, universal church, with the result that this greeting becomes for him the earliest acknowledgment of the primacy of the church of Rome in relation to all other local churches.[5] In contrast, authors such as Adolf Harnack,

---

[5] "The significance of this salutation cannot be overestimated; it is the

followed by Robert Eno, prefer to understand "love" as referring to the well-known generosity of the Christian community in Rome, a trait that continued to be acknowledged in later letters such as those by Dionysius of Corinth in 170 (*Ecclesiastical History* 4.23) and by Dionysius of Alexandria in 256 (ibid., 7.5).[6] In this second view, the Roman church is simply being praised because of its outstanding charity. It probably is not possible to arrive at certainty about the precise meaning that Ignatius intended by this phrase. Quasten's view strikes one as exaggerating its significance at least to some degree; that of Harnack and Eno seems minimizing. Perhaps the truth lies somewhere in between. Indeed, if charity is ultimately the inner soul of all outward ecclesial communion and structure, then perhaps these two interpretations need not be seen as mutually exclusive but rather as complementary.

Irenaeus, for his part, mentions the succession of the bishops of Rome in his argument against the heretics. Orthodox Christian faith is that which is believed in those "apostolic" churches, founded by the apostles. To discover which churches are apostolic, one need simply consult the lists of the bishops of any given community, to see if their succession goes back to the apostles. This leads Irenaeus to provide one of the most important witnesses about how Christians of the second century viewed the church of Rome. "Since it would be very tedious to reckon up the successions of all the churches," he offers to produce only the line of succession "of the very great, the very ancient and universally known church founded and organized at Rome by the two most glorious apostles, Peter and Paul" (*Against the Heresies* 3.3.2).[7]

---

earliest avowal of the Primacy of Rome, that we possess from the pen of a non-Roman ecclesiastic" (J. Quasten, *Patrology*, [Westminster: Newman Press, 1951], 1:68–69).

[6] Eno, *Rise of the Papacy*, 35.

[7] English translation taken from *The Ante-Nicene Fathers*, Vol. 1 (Grand Rapids: Eerdmans, 1975; orig. 1867), 415.

Furthermore, "with this church, by reason of its more excellent origin (*propter potentiorem principalitatem*) every church must agree (*convenire*), i.e. the faithful from everywhere—in which always to the benefit of these people from all over, the tradition which comes from the apostles has been preserved."[8] There follow the names of all of the individuals who led the church in Rome from the mid-sixties, when Peter and Paul were martyred during Nero's persecution, to Eleuterius, bishop of Rome at the time when Irenaeus was writing.

What does Irenaeus mean when he says that every church

---

[8] Here I am following the translation given by Eno (*Rise of the Papacy*, 39), which seems closer to the original as presented in *Sources chrétiennes* 211 (Paris: Cerf, 1974), 32–33. It should be admitted that some object to translating the word *convenire* with the verb "to agree." A. Cleveland Coxe, American editor of *The Ante-Nicene Fathers*, Vol. 1 (pp. 415 and 460–61), translates it as "to resort," construing the whole text to mean that, because of its principal position within the Roman Empire, Rome is a crossroads for Christian believers from the whole known world. It is not that the faith of the church of Rome emanates outward toward all the other churches, but rather that the faithful from all of the churches are obliged to resort or to pass through Rome, with the result that the church of Rome reflects the apostolic traditions that are preserved throughout the whole world. Coxe thinks that his interpretation shows Vatican I's view of papal primacy to be diametrically opposed to Irenaeus's intention and to the correct translation of the text. Coxe's adamancy in denying authority to the Roman church seems to run counter to the evident thrust of Irenaeus's argument. The latter is seeking to identify apostolic churches on the basis of their lists of episcopal succession. Why should Irenaeus, at the very heart of his demonstration that one particular church is apostolic, suddenly shift gears and theorize about the effect that Rome's status as a crossroads has upon the representative quality of her faith? For this reason and because of its clearly apologetic motivation, it seems justified to set aside Coxe's suggestion and to follow instead Eno's translation of *convenire* as "to agree." In principle, however, the idea that the faith of the Roman community might be particularly reflective of the universal church because many believers passed through that city need not contradict the fact that Rome could enjoy a special authority because of its apostolic origin. I would think that the "crossroads" theory would only tend to further enhance the credibility of the faith of the Roman church.

must agree (*necesse est . . . convenire*) with the church in
Rome? Is he simply stating a factual consequence of his
premise that all apostolic churches preserve the same apostolic faith? Since the church in Rome is undeniably apostolic,
and in an unusually strong way, all other apostolic churches
will naturally be in agreement with it. Or does he intend to
say that any church that wishes to conserve the apostolic
faith must conform its belief to that of the Roman church?
In that case, the text would suggest not merely a factual
agreement but a certain obligation to be in harmony with the
teaching of the church in Rome. One factor that could help
in deciding between these options is the reason Irenaeus
gives for this necessity: on account of Rome's "more excellent origin." Here he is more explicit than Clement or
Ignatius in pointing to Peter and Paul as the origin of the
church of Rome. This origin is surely to be understood in a
temporal sense; after mentioning it Irenaeus produces the list
of bishops running from Linus until his own day. But *princi-
palitas* can also connote other meanings, such as the idea of
"source" and therefore also of "authority." Therefore, Irenaeus may intend not only to affirm the temporal credentials
of Rome but also to say that this church enjoys a preeminent
apostolic authority.[9] If this were the case, then the agreement
with Rome's faith would not simply be the logical consequence of Irenaeus's premise that apostolic churches are in
agreement and Rome is an apostolic church. Rather it would
have more the sense of a duty incumbent upon the other
churches. Because of a unique relation to the two great apostles of the New Testament, the church in Rome enjoyed a
unique quality in preserving their message intact.

---

[9] Dominic Unger surveys the remarkable number of interpretations
given to Irenaeus's text in "St. Irenaeus and the Roman Primacy," *Theological Studies* 13 (1952): 359–418, and "St. Irenaeus on the Roman Primacy," *Laurentianum* 4 (1975): 431–45. A more recent analysis of this
passage is given by Roch Kereszty, in *Peter & Paul in the Church of Rome*,
53–69.

It is not possible here to resolve all the questions concerning the correct interpretation of Irenaeus's text. But perhaps that is not necessary. Some preeminence is clearly assigned to the church in Rome on account of its unique relation to Peter and Paul, who, on any account, would have to be considered the principal apostles, and whose presence, after that of Jesus himself, dominates the New Testament. Moreover, they can be said to have "founded" the church in Rome, not by being the first ones to preach there and thus to bring that community to life, but rather by giving their ultimate witness there. They came to stay. In the bosom of this community, they announced the gospel even to the point of shedding their blood. Eusebius tells of a Roman presbyter named Caius who claimed: "But I can point out the trophies of the Apostles. For if you are willing to go to the Vatican or the Ostian Way, you will find the trophies of those who founded this Church" (*Ecclesiastical History* 2.25). To this, Tertullian adds:

> How fortunate is this church into which the apostles poured forth all their teaching along with their blood, where Peter is made equal to the suffering of the Lord, where Paul is rewarded by the death of John [the Baptist], from where the apostle John, after being immersed into boiling oil without suffering, is exiled onto an island. (*Prescription against the Heretics* 36.3)

Tertullian was a lawyer and liked to have the necessary three witnesses prescribed by the book of Deuteronomy, so as to really nail his argument down; that is why he added John. William Farmer sums it up in this way:

> The Neronian persecution devastated the Christian community in Rome. Those who survived were deeply moved by the witness of those sisters and brothers who had been obedient unto death, and above all by the inspiring examples of the apostles Peter and Paul. After the Neronian persecution, the church in Rome was forever to be a church of the martyrs. No theology or *regula* or canon of scriptures would be accepted in this church which did not continue to support,

inspire and hold high the martyriological traditions stemming from Jerusalem and above all the example of the
Master martyr.[10]

Successor to Peter?

There seems little doubt that the Roman church enjoyed a
special religious and spiritual relevance because of this connection with the martyrdom of and the monuments to Peter
and Paul. But would the bishop of Rome at this time also be
viewed as the "successor to Peter," upon whom Jesus stated
he would found his church (Matt. 16:17–19)? Tertullian
seems to be the first to quote this text directly and with some
frequency.[11] In his *Prescription against the Heretics*, he
argues against the Gnostic view that the apostles did not
know all of Jesus' doctrine: "Could anything be hidden from
Peter, the one called the rock on which the church was to be
built, who received the keys of the kingdom of heaven and
the power to loose and bind in heaven and on earth?" (§22).
He also seems to be the origin of that idea, so strong in the
Northern African tradition, which places Peter as the first to
whom was given the power of the keys, which would subsequently be shared with the apostles and with the bishops.

But did Tertullian see the bishop of Rome as embodying
in some way this role of Peter? Probably it is still too early
for such an identification. By emphasizing the foundational
character of Peter he is preparing the way for the future,
when the precise question will be asked: Is there a local
church that in a unique way may be said to be the church of
Peter? The insistence that the bishop of the city where Peter
ministered and gave his final testimony is "successor to
Peter" in a unique way and charged with a unique Petrine

---

[10] Farmer, in *Peter & Paul in the Church of Rome*, 13.

[11] For various texts, see Roland Minnerath, "La position de l'église de
Rome aux trois premiers siècles," in *Il primato del Vescovo di Roma nel
Primo Millennio* (Vatican City: Libreria Editrice Vaticana, 1991), 158.

responsibility becomes an important theme only after the First Council of Constantinople (381), whose third canon claimed a special honor for the bishop of that city simply on the basis of its standing as the "new Rome" or eastern capital of the empire. The bishops of Rome vigorously opposed this claim, arguing that the primatial structuring of the church could not be grounded in merely political factors. Essential ecclesial structures must in some way be rooted in the foundation of the church by Christ.

Early Examples of "Primatial" Leadership

Did the bishops of Rome exercise a role of leadership within the wider "catholic" community during these early centuries? Aside from Clement's letter to the Corinthians, which, without minimizing the caveats mentioned above, still counts as evidence that the pastoral concern of the Roman church extended beyond the limits of its own local community, two other interventions are of importance. The first is the initiative of Victor (189–199) to press for unified practice regarding the celebration of Easter.[12] Some churches, especially in the western part of Asia Minor, followed the ancient custom of celebrating Easter on the 14th day of Nisan (hence the name, "quattordecimans" = 14), whichever day of the week that happened to be. Rome, along with most other local communities, maintained that Easter should be celebrated on Sunday, the day of the Lord's resurrection. Eusebius records that a series of regional synods were held— in Palestine, Rome, Pontus, Gaul, Osrhoene [Northwest Mesopotamia, encompassing the city of Edessa], and Corinth, all of which agreed that Easter should be celebrated on the Lord's Day. Polycrates of Ephesus, however, on behalf

---

[12] It has been proposed that Eusebius was seriously mistaken in reading his sources, mistaking a local controversy about the celebration of Easter within the very cosmopolitan Christian community at Rome for a worldwide controversy. Eno nicely points out the values and limitations of this proposal (*Rise of the Papacy*, 41–42).

of the bishops of Asia Minor, wrote to Victor informing him that they would continue to observe Easter on the fourteenth day of Nisan, since it was their ancient practice and many apostles and saints from the earliest Christian generations had done so. Polycrates wrote: "I am not frightened at what is threatened us, for those greater than I have said, 'We ought to obey God rather than men' (Acts 5:29)" (*Ecclesiastical History* 5.24). What had been threatened becomes immediately clear when Eusebius reports that Victor tried to excommunicate these churches. Not all of the other bishops went along with this, some writing to Victor, encouraging him to relent. Among these was Irenaeus, whose letter, conserved in Eusebius's history, is a wonderful testimony in favor of ecclesial unity which allows for diversity. If we remain in communion, urges Irenaeus, the very disagreement about when to end the Lenten fast will confirm our fundamental unanimity in faith. He further recalls that, decades earlier (ca. 155), the famous bishop Polycarp of Smyrna had visited his Roman counterpart Anicetus (155–166) to discuss the same question. While in the end they did not agree, nevertheless they parted in peace, Anicetus inviting Polycarp to preside at the Eucharist that they shared before Polycarp returned to Smyrna and, as it turned out, to his own martyrdom.

This episode undeniably shows that the Roman bishop enjoyed a certain prestige among the bishops throughout the world. In addition, some type of "primatial authority" may be divined in the fact that the synod in Asia Minor seems to have been held at Victor's request (Polycrates writes to Victor of "the bishops . . . whom you requested to be summoned by me"). It also shows Rome's interest in promoting a unified liturgical practice within the Christian community as a whole, as well as its awareness of itself as competent to excommunicate an entire group of local churches who did not accept the more common practice. At the same time, the Easter controversy shows that the holding of various synods went hand in hand with the personal intervention of the bishop of Rome and, moreover, that his action was not simply accepted by the other churches.[13] Indeed, many bishops responded by advising Victor to modify his own seemingly rather harsh position.

A second major churchwide crisis in which the bishop of Rome played a significant role during the pre-Nicaean period was the controversy over the lapsed. The issue here concerned the reconciliation of those Christians who, out of fear for their life or safety during the brutal persecution that began under the emperor Decius in 249, had offered sacrifice to the Roman gods or had procured documents that falsely testified that they had so sacrificed. It would be difficult to overstate the trauma caused for the church by Decius's reign of terror. It led to a huge number of defections and precipitated the problem of reconciliation between those who had remained faithful and those who had lapsed, once the persecutions had run their course.[14] While some bishops were relatively lenient in readmitting the lapsed and some "confessors," survivors of torture during the persecution who consequently enjoyed great prestige within the Christian community, wrote letters on behalf of those who had fallen requesting lenience, other bishops required a rigorous period of public penance prior to full reintegration into the church. Originally Cyprian of Carthage and the newly elected bishop of Rome, Cornelius (251–253), whom Cyprian had supported in his struggle against the anti-pope Novatian, agreed on a somewhat moderate position. They opposed the rigorists who completely refused reconciliation to the lapsed, but they were also against excessive lenience.

This harmony between the two sees, however, would prove to be short-lived. Cornelius was quickly succeeded in

---

[13] Roch Kereszty writes: "Thus Victor's activity reveals both an awareness of his authority to decide who belongs to the universal church but also a policy of collegial action, consulting with his brother bishops before making a decision" (*Peter & Paul in the Church of Rome*, 67).

[14] See G. Bardy, "La grande crise du IIIe siècle," in his *La Théologie de l'Église de saint Irénée au concile de Nicée*, Unam Sanctam 14 (Paris: Cerf, 1947), 167–251.

Rome by Lucius (253–254) and then by Stephen (254–257).
Soon a disagreement arose regarding the validity of baptisms
celebrated by clergy who had lapsed during the persecution
or by heretics. Stephen, appealing to the tradition, believed
that such baptisms were valid but ineffective; should those
so baptized seek full integration into the church, only the
laying on of hands, the rite associated with the reconciliation
of penitents, would be required. Most of the bishops of
Alexandria and Palestine agreed with him. Cyprian, on the
other hand, along with the bishops of Africa and those
within the orbit of Antioch, were convinced that heretics or
the lapsed were incapable of baptizing, being themselves outside of the church. Converts from such communities had to
be rebaptized, or, rather, baptized for the first time. The controversy never really was resolved, and Stephen and Cyprian
were both martyred within a few years (by 258), not having
been reconciled, although the degree to which they were formally out of communion with each other remains unclear.

But this controversial situation gave rise to several letters
that provide interesting information about relations between
bishops in the mid-third century.[15] One is from the year 254,
in which Cyprian and a large number of bishops of Africa
respond to an appeal by the Spanish communities of Leon
and Astorga. Apparently their bishops, Basilides and
Martial, had escaped persecution by obtaining certificates
attesting that they had sacrificed to the idols. They were subsequently deposed by their communities and replaced by
new bishops. However, Basilides repented and appealed to
Stephen, bishop of Rome, asking to be reinstated. Stephen
supported Basilides, which prompted the Spanish communities then to write to Cyprian requesting the help of the
church in North Africa against Basilides. The Africans
obliged. Cyprian and his fellow bishops backed the deposi-

---

[15] The letters to be considered here are all found in the collection
assigned to Cyprian, some of which, of course, were written not by him
but by others and addressed to him.

tion of the two lapsed bishops, excusing Stephen on the grounds that he was too far from the scene to really know the facts of the case; he evidently had been tricked by Basilides, making the latter's crime all the greater. Cyprian's letter appeals to the decree that an earlier bishop of Rome, Cornelius, had made, with the agreement of all the bishops of the world, that such repentant bishops could be readmitted to the church as penitents but not as ordained ministers (*Letter 67* 5–6). This letter contains some very revealing information. Evidently a Spanish bishop felt he could appeal to the bishop of Rome to overturn the sentence he received from his own community, and the bishop of Rome felt authorized to support him against that local decision. At the same time, the church in Africa felt no hesitation to resist the action of Rome's bishop, appealing, nevertheless, to the collegially made decision of an earlier bishop of Rome!

Another revealing letter is from Cyprian to Stephen about Marcian, the bishop of Arles. The problem was the opposite of that raised in the case of the Spanish bishops. Marcian was a rigorist and had begun to refuse reconciliation under any circumstance to the lapsed of his diocese. "Many of our brethren have died there in recent years without peace," writes Cyprian: "let relief come to the rest who remain alive and groan both day and night and, beseeching the divine and paternal mercy, ask the solace of our help" (*Letter 68* 3). Cyprian advises Stephen to "write a very full letter to our fellow bishops abiding in Gaul," telling them that Marcian should be excommunicated and another elected in his place (*Letter 68* 2). The letter also includes a lovely affirmation about episcopal responsibility for the one church spread throughout the whole world: "For although we shepherds are many, yet we feed one flock; and all of the sheep whom Christ sought by His Blood and Passion we ought to collect and to cherish and not to allow our suppliant and grieving brothers to be cruelly despised and to be trodden under foot by the proud presumption of certain ones . . ." (*Letter 68* 4).

Again some fascinating questions are raised. Why could

not the bishops of Gaul have acted upon their own in resolving the problem of Marcian? Or why would not a letter to them from Cyprian have been sufficient encouragement? Why is it so important precisely that Stephen intervene? In addition, Cyprian's complaint almost seems to run counter to his position in the case of the Spanish bishops, where he was displeased with Stephen's intervention as being too lenient. Now the complaint is that the Roman bishop has not intervened on behalf of leniency and in opposition to the excessive rigorism of the bishop of Arles. Obviously Cyprian's letter presupposes that the bishop of Rome has a (unique?) responsibility to intervene when difficulties disturb a particular local church. Yet this role of the Roman bishop is contextualized by the affirmation of the responsibility of the entire group of bishops for the welfare of the one unique flock united throughout the world. Cyprian is sometimes characterized as the champion of the ecclesiology of the local church and of the local bishop. While this is true, it should not obscure his awareness of and sense of responsibility for the "catholic" church as a whole.

Two years later, in 256, a third letter, again critical of Stephen, was received by Cyprian from Firmilian, the bishop of Caesarea in Cappadocia, where one hundred years later St. Basil the Great would be bishop. Now the problem was precisely the question of the validity of baptism administered by heretics. Stephen had argued that the tradition going back to the apostles mandated that, where the proper procedure for baptism had been followed, the baptism should be considered valid. Firmilian responds quite harshly: "no one is so stupid as to believe that the apostles handed this down since it is certainly evident that these very detestable and execrable heresies arose later since even Marcion" (*Letter 75* 5). Stephen's behavior among the churches is called audacious and insolent (*Letter 75* 3). The bishop of Caesarea recalls that the Roman church had already shown itself unfaithful to the tradition handed down from the beginning concerning the celebration of Easter (*Letter 75* 6); evidently the sting of

Victor's threat to excommunicate the churches of Asia Minor still smarted, some sixty years later. Firmilian's many arguments can be fairly represented with that drawn from Eph. 4:5, which affirms that there is "one Lord, one faith, one baptism." These three go together. To recognize the baptism of the heretics is *ipso facto* to place oneself in communion with them in faith (*Letter 75* 25).

Foundations upon the Rock

In the midst of this discussion of baptism, Firmilian makes several statements that are relevant to church order. He recalls that Christ founded the one and only church upon the rock, when he "said to Peter alone: 'Whatever thou shalt bind on earth shall be bound also in heaven . . .'" (16). He then adds:

> And I am justly indignant in this respect at this so open and manifest stupidity of Stephen that he who so glories in the place of his episcopate and contends that he has the succession from Peter, on whom the foundations of the Church were established, should introduce many other rocks and constitute new buildings of many churches while he maintains by his authority that baptism is there. For they who are baptized fill up without doubt the number of the Church. . . . Stephen, who claims that through succession he has the See of Peter, is stirred up with no zeal against the heretics. . . . (17)

Apparently the notion that the unity of the church was tied to the fact that it had been founded upon Peter alone was not peculiar to Tertullian and, as we shall see, Cyprian. Firmilian is from Cappadocia in Asia Minor. But there is something more here. He notes that Stephen claims to have, through succession, the very see of Peter. Firmilian does not dispute this claim, but rather chides Stephen for not being correspondingly zealous against the heretics. This seems to be a recognition that the bishop of Rome is successor to Peter in a way different from other bishops, that is, he succeeds to

Peter's own see. One glimpses a similar acknowledgment in the earlier letter (252) of Cyprian to Stephen's predecessor Cornelius. Apparently Cyprian's enemies had sent emissaries to Rome to appeal actions which he had taken against them in Carthage. Cyprian warns Cornelius not to receive them, adding that "they dare to sail and to bring letters from the heretics and blasphemers to the Chair of Peter and to the principal Church whence sacerdotal unity has sprung, and not to think that those are the Romans whose faith was praised by the Apostle preaching; to them perfidy cannot have access" (*Letter 59* 14). He adds a reaffirmation of the authority of the local church: offenses should be judged in the place where they occurred and the authority of the bishops in Africa is perfectly adequate to deal with the questions which arise there. But there seems to be an undeniable identification here between the "chair of Peter" and the see to which these heretics sailed to make their appeal, the see of Rome. Moreover, this church is called the "principal church whence sacerdotal unity has sprung" (*ecclesia principalis unde unitas sacerdotalis exorta est*).[16]

Finally, a word should be said about the little book occasioned by the troubles that Cyprian and Cornelius had in maintaining unity within their respective local churches. Chapters 4 and 5 of Cyprian's *On the Unity of the Catholic Church* (251) are especially pertinent to the question of primacy. In chapter 4, after recalling the text in which Jesus founds the church on Peter and gives him the keys of the kingdom (Matt. 16:18–19), Cyprian turns to the scene in which the risen Lord bestows the Holy Spirit upon the apostles along with the power to forgive sins (John 20:21–23). He sees the sequence of these events as having an ecclesiological significance for the unity of the church. Although, after the resurrection, Jesus

---

[16] A fine essay showing the resonance between this text and others, both by Cyprian and by other patristic writers, is Pierre Batiffol, "Ecclesia Principalis," in his *Cathedra Petri*, Unam Sanctam 4 (Paris: Cerf, 1938), 135–50.

bestows equal power upon all the Apostles . . . yet that He might display unity, He established by His authority the origin of the same unity as beginning from one. Surely the rest of the Apostles also were that which Peter was, endowed with an equal partnership of office and of power, but the beginning proceeds from unity, that the church of Christ may be shown to be one.[17]

Two versions of chapter 4 have been preserved. The one not quoted contains the following variations, which are usually thought to be more favorable to the primacy of the bishop of Rome. Jesus set up but one chair (*unam tamen cathedram constituit*); the primacy is given to Peter (*primatus Petro datur*) and the unity of the church is demonstrated by the unity of the chair (*et una ecclesia et cathedra una monstratur*).[18] Cyprian asks rhetorically: How could one who does not maintain unity with Peter presume to have kept the faith? How could one who abandons the chair of Peter (*cathedra Petri*) presume to be in the church, which is founded upon that chair?

The fact that two versions have survived has generated much discussion. Earlier commentators presupposed that the text more favorable to the primacy must have been a later forgery, consisting of interpolations added by some author who wished to show that even Cyprian favored the primacy of the bishop of Rome. More recent scholarship has shown the truth to be just the opposite. M. Bévenot seems to have won the day with his argument that the text more favorable to primacy was in fact the earlier of the two and that Cyprian himself, after his dispute with Stephen, rewrote the chapter, deleting the various references to the "cathedra" of Peter, which could too easily be identified with the see of Rome.[19]

---

[17] Translation of Roy J. Deferrari, taken from *Saint Cyprian: Treatises*, The Fathers of the Church 36 (Washington, D.C.: Catholic University of America Press, 1958), 98–99.

[18] See M. Bévenot, "'Primatus Petro datur': St. Cyprian on the Papacy," *Journal of Theological Studies* n.s. 5 (1954): 19–35.

[19] Bévenot's position is briefly stated in his introduction to the *De*

Whatever the case may be regarding the sequence and motivation of the changes to chapter 4, Bévenot argues that there is a fundamental continuity between the two versions. That the more "primatial" version (the one with the references to the *cathedra Petri*) included the affirmations about the episcopacy which immediately follow in chapter 5 of both versions:

> This unity we ought to hold firmly and defend, especially we bishops who watch over the Church, that we may prove that also the episcopate itself is one and undivided. Let no one deceive the brotherhood by lying; let no one corrupt the faith by a perfidious prevarication of the truth. The episcopate is one, the parts of which are held together by the individual bishops [*Episcopatus unus est cuius a singulis in solidum pars tenetur*].[20]

Cyprian has far too great an appreciation of the responsibility of the episcopacy for the welfare of the whole church and of the dignity of the office of each individual bishop to subscribe to any view that would somehow diminish the bishops by exalting the primacy. These words from the opening of chapter 5 of *On the Unity of the Catholic Church* reaffirm this appreciation of the dignity and unity of the episcopacy. This dignity is also captured in a refrain that recurs through many of Cyprian's letters, that is, that each bishop ultimately must answer to God alone for his actions. Examples:

> While the bond of concord remains and the indivisible rite of the Catholic Church continues, each bishop disposes and directs his own work as one who will render an account of his purpose to the Lord. (Letter 55 21 [Cyprian to Bishop Antonian, late 251 or 252])

Ecclesiae Catholicae Unitate, in *Sancti Cypriani Episcopi Opera*, Corpus Christianorum Series Latina, III (Turnhout: Brepols, 1972), 244–47. The Latin quoted here is taken from pp. 251–52 of the Corpus Christianorum version.

[20] On the last sentence here quoted, see M. Bévenot, "In solidum and St. Cyprian: A Correction (De unitate Ecclesiae, V)," *Journal of Theological Studies* n.s. 6 (1955): 244–48.

And:

> . . . every prelate who will render an account of his actions to
> the Lord, should decide what he thinks best, according to
> what the blessed Apostle Paul writes in his Epistle to the
> Romans and says: "Every one of us will render an account
> for himself. Therefore let us not judge one another" (Rom.
> 14:12–13). (*Letter 69* 17 [Cyprian to Magnus, 255]; see also
> *Letter 72* 3 [Cyprian to Stephen, 255] and *Letter 73* 26
> [Cyprian to Jubaian, 256])

The council of the eighty-seven bishops, held in Carthage in
258 in response to a letter by Stephen condemning the
decrees of the African council on the baptism of heretics,
seemed to apply this general principle to the relations
between bishops.

> . . . each of us should bring forward what we think, judging
> no man, nor rejecting any one from the right of communion,
> if he should think differently from us. For neither does any of
> us set himself up as a bishop of bishops, nor by tyrannical
> terror does any compel his colleague to the necessity of obe-
> dience; since every bishop, according to the allowance of his
> liberty and power, has his own proper right of judgment, and
> can no more be judged by another than he himself can judge
> another. But let us all wait for the judgment of our Lord Jesus
> Christ, who is the only one that has the power both of pre-
> ferring us in the government of His Church, and of judging
> us in our conduct there.[21]

Of course, such an individualistic vision of the account-
ability of each bishop did not prove workable, even as the
letters of Cyprian himself show. Moreover, even the less primatial version of chapter 4 of *On the Unity of the Catholic
Church* places the accent upon the unity of the origin of the
episcopacy which prevents any radical individualism on the
part of the bishops. Though all the apostles enjoyed "equal
power" and "were that which Peter was, endowed with an

---

[21] In *Ante-Nicene Fathers*, vol. 5 (Grand Rapids: Eerdmans, 1975), 565.

equal partnership of office and of power," nevertheless Jesus "established by his authority the origin of the same unity as beginning from one." We see Cyprian holding together both the dignity of each and the unity of all. It is not an easy balance to maintain. Part of the maintenance of this balance, even for Cyprian, fell to the helpful interventions of the bishop of Rome.

In the earliest centuries of the life of the church not all of the events that could have some relevance for our present investigation were recorded. The last such recorded event that occurred prior to the council of Nicaea (325) helps to explain that council's sixth canon, the first text in history that actually uses the word "primacy" in relation to the ministry of the Roman bishop.[22] It occurred about ten years after the death of Cyprian, when a synod held in Antioch deposed that city's bishop, Paul of Samosata. The synod wrote to the bishops of Alexandria and Rome, asking them to confirm the deposition of Paul and to recognize the new bishop who had been elected in his place. The interesting implication of this letter is that a synod from such a great city as Antioch, which, along with Rome, Alexandria, Carthage, Ephesus, and Corinth, was one of the most often mentioned in Eusebius's *Ecclesiastical History*, could not, of its own authority, depose its bishop, whom it had judged to be heretical, and confirm his replacement. It felt it necessary to gain the recognition and agreement of the other great sees. In 325, at the Council of Nicaea, the three churches whose special primacy in their particular regions was acknowledged were precisely the sees mentioned in Eusebius's account of the deposition of Paul of Samosata: Alexandria, Antioch, and Rome.

---

[22] J. Ratzinger so identifies Nicaea's sixth canon and comments at greater length about the material I have synthesized in the rest of this paragraph (*Das Neue Volk Gottes* [Düsseldorf: Patmos, 1969], 122–26).

CHAPTER 3

"Peter Has Spoken through Leo": The Era of the Great Ecumenical Councils

Constantine and the First Two Ecumenical Councils

When Constantine the Great defeated Maxentius in 312 at the Milvian Bridge over the Tiber River, just north of Rome, he did not thereby become the sole ruler of the Roman Empire. He still shared the leadership with his fellow "Augustus" in charge of the eastern territories, Licinius. It was together with Licinius that he issued, the following year, the edict of Milan, granting toleration to the Christian religion. Toleration did not mean full-scale adoption. In fact, at first the majority of the population of the empire continued to adhere to the ancient pagan religion that Rome had inherited in large part from the Greeks. Constantine was in no position to outlaw its rites and practices. Indeed he expressly allowed the celebration of its feasts and did not himself accept baptism until he was close to death, even though ecclesiastical authors like Eusebius vigorously attest that he was a sincere Christian believer right from the time of his victory over Maxentius. The concluding paragraphs of Eusebius's *Ecclesiastical History* report the event that finally gave the government of the whole empire to Constantine alone: his defeat of Licinius in the naval battle at Chrysopolis, near Byzantium, in 324. Four years later he broke the ground for a new capital in the East, which he planned to build upon the small, seventh-century B.C. town of Byzantium and which was to be called the "city of Constantine," Constantinople.

51

Both Constantine's embrace of Christianity and his foundation of a new capital would occasion significant developments in relations between the bishops and, in particular, in the distinctive exercise of the authority of the bishop of Rome. As emperor, Constantine was a figure whose interests and responsibility encompassed the whole known world. Moreover, within the Roman Empire, religion had always been considered a matter of vital importance to the state. The persecutions of Christians, the last of which was begun as recently as the final years of the reign of the emperor Diocletian (285–305), demonstrated just how important it was thought to be. Toleration did not mean that religion no longer mattered but rather that the emperor would now consider the well-being of the Christian community as a matter of interest to the state. In fact, hardly was the ink dry on the edict of toleration when a group of bishops from the Numidian province of Northern Africa appealed to the emperor in their effort to oust the newly elected bishop of Carthage, Caecilian, whose consecration, they alleged, was tainted by the participation of a bishop who had lapsed during the persecution of Diocletian.[1] Eusebius preserves a letter from Constantine to the bishop of Rome, Miltiades (311–314), directing him to hold a synod to consider the case against Caecilian (*Ecclesiastical History* 10.5). Actually several such synods were held, the most famous one being the Council of Arles in 314, attended by thirty-four bishops from the western half of the empire. These synods all opposed the position of the donatists, both in principle and in the particular case of Caecilian.

---

[1] This group would be led eventually by a priest, then bishop, named Donatus. What became known in later history as "donatism," the rigorous view that the validity of the celebration of sacraments depended on the holiness of the minister, survived persecution by the now Christian empire as well as the opposition of such a major figure as St. Augustine of Hippo, only to die out slowly with the rest of the Christian community of North Africa after the coming of the Muslims in the seventh century.

But more important to our purposes than the decision about donatism is the very fact of the intervention of the emperor in directing a bishop of Rome to organize a council to deal with a matter internal to the church. Such an initiative by the emperor would very soon occur again, now not in response to a regional problem but to a question relevant to the Christian community as a whole: the teachings of Arius concerning the subordination of the Son of God to the Father. Not only did the first ecumenical council of Nicaea (325) achieve the important doctrinal clarification that the Son is "of one substance" with the Father, but it also gave the first series of twenty "canons" (laws, rules) to govern the life of the church throughout the world. The sixth of these is entitled: "Concerning the forms of primacy belonging to some cities; and that bishops may not be created without the consent of the metropolitan." This first canon about "primacy" reads as follows:

> The ancient customs of Egypt, Libya and Pentapolis shall be maintained, according to which the bishop of Alexandria has authority over all these places, since a similar custom exists with reference to the bishop of Rome. Similarly in Antioch and the other provinces the prerogatives of the churches are to be preserved.
>
> In general the following principle is evident: if anyone is made bishop without the consent of the metropolitan, this great synod determines that such a one shall not be a bishop. If however two or three by reason of personal rivalry dissent from the common vote of all, provided it is reasonable and in accordance with the Church's canon, the vote of the majority shall prevail.[2]

Several details of this text immediately jump out as relevant for our study. First of all, it is clear that, at the time of the first ecumenical council, in no part of the church did the

---

[2] Translation taken from Norman P. Tanner, ed., *Decrees of the Ecumenical Councils* (Washington, D.C.: Georgetown University Press, 1990), 1:8–9.

bishops comprise a wholly homogeneous and undifferenti-
ated group, all of them simply being equal and none of them
exercising a role of leadership in relation to the others. Such
unqualified equality is excluded by the requirement of the
consent of the metropolitan for the consecration of new
bishops. Of course, the respect that this canon shows for dis-
senting bishops and its rule of honoring a vote of the majority constitute an important recognition of the fundamental
equality among them. But the metropolitan system of orga-
nizing a number of bishops around one principal bishop presupposes a certain hierarchical order among the bishops.
Some exercise a role of leadership and of authority in foster-
ing unity among the others who belong to the same ecclesiastical territory.[3]

Second, the text states that, just as Alexandria "has authority over" Egypt, Libya, and Pentapolis, so too do Rome
and Antioch exercise a unique authority in their particular
regions. The area attributed to Alexandria is considerably
larger than the size of a metropolitan region. Apparently the
same was implied for the other two as well; they were not
being singled out merely for being metropolitan sees.[4] It
should be noted that Nicaea here speaks not of one but of

---

[3] Particularly dear to Orthodox thought about ecclesial organization is
the famous "Canon 34 of the Apostles." The origins of this canon derive
already from the fourth century, but it was formally adopted at the Quinisext Synod of 691, also called the synod in Trullo, which approved 102
disciplinary canons, much needed because the fifth and sixth (hence
"Quinisext") ecumenical councils had only treated doctrinal questions.
The text of Canon 34 reads: "It is necessary that the bishops of each
nation know who among them holds the first place and that they consider
him as their head. They should not do anything without his consent, even
though it belongs to each one to deal with the problems of his own diocese and of the territory in his care. But also the primate should do nothing without the consent of all the others. In this way, peace will reign and
God will be glorified through Christ in the Holy Spirit." Greek and Latin
versions can be found in C. Kirch, *Enchiridion Fontium Historiae Ecclesiasticae Antiquae* (Barcelona: Herder, 1960), nos. 697, 408.

[4] The suburbicarian region over which the bishop of Rome would seem

three "primacies." Canon 7 adds that Jerusalem is worthy of special honor, "saving the dignity which is proper to the metropolitan" of the region. Though the city of Jesus' ministry and death, Jerusalem was a suffragan diocese to the see of Caesarea. Why do Alexandria, Rome, and Antioch enjoy a special authority over rather vast areas of the church? Nicaea simply attributes this to "ancient custom." Evidently the bishops of these cities had exercised such a primatial authority in their respective areas and this authority had been acknowledged by the other local churches for quite a long time prior to 325.

It was only after the Council of Nicaea that the new capital of Constantinople was dedicated in the year 330. The very next ecumenical council would be held in this new imperial city in 381 and would deal with an issue somewhat similar to that of its predecessor: whereas Nicaea had made use of the word *homoousios* to affirm the divinity of the Son, the First Council of Constantinople (I Constantinople) expanded the third section of Nicaea's creed in order to assert unequivocally the divinity of the Holy Spirit. But perhaps of equal or even greater significance was the fact that I Constantinople confirmed the trinitarian and christological doctrine of Nicaea. The doctrine that the Son was "of the same substance" as the Father had not been received easily by the churches in the East. This was due not only to the difficult philosophical and theological questions it raised but perhaps even more to the personal ties between Arius and such prominent bishops as Eusebius of Nicomedia, as well as to the pro-Arian leanings of several emperors. In the very complex sequence of events during the fifty-six years sepa-

---

to exercise a regional primacy analogous to that which Alexandria exercised in its region is succinctly described by C. Vogel, "Unité de l'Église et pluralité des formes historiques d'organisation ecclésiastique du IIIe au Ve siècle," in *L'Épiscopat et l'Église universelle*, ed. Y. Congar and B. D. Dupuy, Unam Sanctam 39 (Paris: Cerf, 1962), 628–29. Also see n. 13 below.

rating the two councils, the most visible champion of Nicaea in the East was Athanasius, bishop of Alexandria from 328 to his death in 373. Five times Athanasius was exiled from his see because of his support of the *homoousios* doctrine; twice he took refuge in the West. When he left Alexandria for the second time in 339, two years after the death of Constantine, his opponents, apparently thinking they could get rid of him permanently, invited the bishop of Rome, Julius I (337–352), to hold a synod to consider the charges against Athanasius. To their surprise, however, Julius and the western bishops were thoroughly in support both of Athanasius and of Nicaea, prompting Eusebius of Nicomedia and his followers to counter with the Dedication Council of Antioch (341), whose creed omitted the *homoousios* formula of Nicaea.

Constantine's sons Constans and Constantius II, who now ruled the western and eastern halves of the empire respectively, convoked a council to attempt to bring the two sides together. This council was held in Sardica in 343 and failed to achieve reconciliation, apparently because some of the eastern bishops refused to sit in a joint meeting with Athanasius and his fellow exiles. However, Sardica did produce several canons that would have no little importance for the unfolding relationship between the bishop of Rome and the other bishops. Canons 3–5 gave any bishop who believed he had been unfairly condemned within his ecclesiastical province the right to initiate an appeal to the bishop of Rome, who, for his part, was not to judge the case himself, but rather was to determine whether a review of the case should take place in the province of the bishop in question. Canon 3 connects this role of the Roman bishop with Peter: ". . . let us honor the memory of Peter the apostle, and let these judges write to Julius the bishop of Rome so that through the bishops who border on the province, if it should be necessary, the trial be reopened, and he himself should furnish the judges." Appealing to Rome in disputed cases was not new; Cyprian's letters give evidence of such appeals at least ninety years earlier. But now this practice receives canonical status from a council that had been intended as a gathering of bishops from both halves of the empire. Later, Roman bishops would more than once mistakenly claim that the ecumenical council of Nicaea had sanctioned and even required the practice of appealing major cases (*causae maiores*) to the bishop of Rome.[5] Actually, these canons came from Sardica, which enjoyed significantly less authority than Nicaea.

The Nicene controversy continued for another thirty-five years. During this time, Julius's successor, Liberius (352– 366), after much resistance and even exile, was finally pressured into agreeing to the deposition of Athanasius, a fact that eventually led to his being considered a heretic by some theologians of the Middle Ages, a rather dubious distinction for a pope. Later, a council was held in Rimini in 359, at which the western bishops as a body, who had always tended to support Nicaea, finally agreed under imperial pressure to accept a non-Nicene creed. The bishop of Rome was not present at that council, a fact that later popes would marshal to support their condemnation of the Rimini council and their contention that no council can be valid without the approval of the bishop of Rome.[6] In the end, it was only

---

[5] Pope Innocent I (401–417) attributes to Nicaea several canons from Sardica about appeal to the bishop of Rome in his letter to the bishop of Rouen: *Epistola II*, 5–6 (Migne, *PL*, 20:472–73). Pope Zosimus (417– 418), of Greek origin, did the same in his *Epistola XV* (Migne, *PL*, 20:681–82), as did Leo I in his letter of October 13, 449 (no. 44) to the emperor Theodosius II, protesting the "robber synod" of Ephesus (in St. Leo the Great, *Letters*, trans. E. Hunt, The Fathers of the Church 34, [Washington, D.C.: Catholic University of America Press, 1957], 122–26, at 126). This latter translation will henceforth be referred to as Hunt, *Letters*, followed by the page number.

[6] Liberius's successor, the Spanish bishop Damasus, held a synod at Rome in 371, which argued that the Arian creed professed by the four hundred western bishops at the synod of Rimini did not express the faith of the church because "neither the bishop of the Romans, whose opinion ought to have been sought before all the others, nor Vincentius [of Capua], who had kept his episcopate untainted so many years, nor the rest gave

with the accession of Theodosius I as emperor in the East, a staunch supporter of Nicaea, and with the short but effective ministry of Gregory of Nazianzus as bishop of Constantinople (379–381), that Arianism was finally defeated, though even then it would not die out completely for some generations, especially among those barbarian invaders whose tribes originally had been evangelized by Arians.

By solemnly reconfirming the orthodoxy of the doctrine of Nicaea, the First Council of Constantinople not only resolved an important question of Christian doctrine, but it also thereby showed ecumenical councils to be a dependable means by which the community could remain faithful to the truth of the gospel. Faith and order went hand in hand. Because they resolved the controversies over the consubstantiality of the Son and the Spirit with the Father, ecumenical councils were recognized by the church as a valid expression of her nature as a communion in faith. Something analogous can also be said of the primatial role of the bishop of Rome. The delegates of the bishop of Rome were not the principal voices during the actual celebration of the Council of Nicaea; nor were his delegates even present at the First Council of Constantinople. But between the two councils, the actions of the bishops of Rome in responding positively to appeals from embattled orthodox bishops such as Athanasius and in defending the doctrine of Nicaea against bishops and councils who opposed it demonstrated the effectiveness of the primatial ministry in promoting the unity of the wider catholic church as a whole. Pope Damasus (366–384) surely would

---

their approval to such doctrine" (in *Patrologiae cursus completus: Series graeca,* ed. J. P. Migne [Paris, 1857–1866], vol. 82, col. 1053; hereafter this series will be referred to as Migne, *PG,* followed by the volume and column numbers). Translation taken from Arthur C. Piepkorn, "The Roman Primacy in the Patristic Era. II, From Nicaea to Leo the Great," in *Papal Primacy and the Universal Church,* ed. Paul C. Empie and T. Austin Murphy, Lutherans and Catholics in Dialogue 5 (Minneapolis: Augsburg, 1974), 73–97 at 81.

have rejoiced at the doctrinal outcome of I Constantinople, for which he and his predecessors had been such a positive force for over half a century. However, he was in for an unpleasant surprise when he read the third canon appended to that council's profession of faith. It read: "Because it is new Rome, the bishop of Constantinople is to enjoy the privileges of honor after the bishop of Rome."

The Petrine Justification of the Primacy

The problem with canon 3 was its apparent deviation from what had been the standard argument supporting authority within the church since the earliest post–New Testament writings. The authority of the bishops had been said to derive ultimately from the mission of the apostles, which in turn was founded on the command of Jesus himself. By calling on the divine origins of the apostolic mission and its continuation in the succession of the bishops, a second-century writer such as Irenaeus was able to work against the splintering of the Christian community into many small, mutually exclusive sects, each justified by its own particular Gnostic privatization of Christian faith. In the third century, Cyprian emphasized the fact that the church was founded upon the apostle Peter in order to argue for the equality and unity of all bishops. It is true that, when canon 6 of Nicaea acknowledged a regional primacy of the bishops of Alexandria, Rome, and Antioch on the basis of "ancient custom," it did not refer explicitly to the apostolic origins of those churches. But neither did it call into question the basic principle that fundamental ecclesial structures need to find their ultimate grounding in such apostolic beginnings and thus, ultimately, in the will of God. In contrast, by elevating to a position above Alexandria and Antioch a city that was only recently founded and did not claim for its church an apostolic origin in the same way that those cities did,[7] I Constantinople's

---

[7] The claim that the ancient city of Byzantium, upon which Constan-

third canon seemed to base primatial authority upon the merely secular circumstance that Constantinople happened to be the new capital of the Roman Empire. Moreover, it presupposed that an ecumenical council enjoyed the authority needed to determine such an issue.

Damasus's response was swift.[8] He held a council the following year which affirmed that Rome's primacy was based not on a decree from any synod but rather on the voice of the Lord in the gospel, when he said, "You are Peter and on this rock I will build my church" (Matt. 16:18–19). Added to this Petrine basis was the fact that the apostle Paul, the "vessel of election," had also consecrated the church of Rome by his glorious death during the persecution of Nero. The synod of Rome concluded:

> The first see of the apostle Peter is therefore the Roman church, "without spot or wrinkle or any such thing" [Eph. 5:27]. But the second see was consecrated at Alexandria, in the name of blessed Peter, by Mark his disciple, the evangelist. He was directed into Egypt by the apostle Peter. . . . The third see of the most blessed apostle Peter is at Antioch, which is held in honor because he initially lived there before he came to Rome and because there the name of the new race of Christians first arose.[9]

Obviously Nicaea's canon 6 about the special role of Alexandria, Rome, and Antioch is reinterpreted here in a Petrine key. Their authority is based not simply on "ancient custom." Rather this custom is itself rooted in the fact that each of these churches could claim to be Peter's, upon whom Jesus founded the church.

---

tinople was founded, was evangelized by the apostle Andrew was not yet put forward at this time. It seems that it was proposed only several centuries later. See F. Dvornik, *The Idea of Apostolicity in Byzantium and the Legend of the Apostle Andrew* (Cambridge, Mass.: Harvard University Press, 1958).

[8] See Piepkorn, "Roman Primacy," 82.

[9] Translation from Piepkorn, "Roman Primacy," 82.

With Damasus, the bishops of Rome became more outspoken in claiming that their primatial role rested upon the
fact that they were successors to Peter. Damasus was followed by Siricius (384–399), who in 385 wrote what has
been called the first papal decretal to Himerius of Tarragona,
a city on the northeast coast of the Iberian peninsula. Himerius had written to Rome for guidance about a series of pastoral questions, such as the rebaptism of Arians, the proper
time within the liturgical year for the celebration of baptism,
the qualities required in the clergy and so forth. Siricius says
that he is able to give direction about such issues to a bishop
in faraway Spain, indeed that he has a duty not to remain
silent, because "we bear the burden of all who are heavily
laden or, rather, the blessed apostle Peter bears them in us,
who in all things, as we trust, protects and defends those
who are heirs of his government."[10] Clearly, in the mind of
Siricius, Peter acts through the bishop of Rome.

In a similar way, Innocent I (401–417) responded to a
request for guidance from the bishops of Macedonia about
various pastoral matters, characterizing his judgment as
coming "from the apostolic mouth" (*ore apostolico*).[11] Innocent's directives to the Macedonian bishops need to be
understood within the context of the peculiar relation
between that area and the bishop of Rome. When, in 379,
the emperor Gratian transferred several provinces that had
been under the western half of the empire (Dacia, Macedonia, and Achaia) to the eastern empire, Pope Damasus
designated one bishop from that region, the bishop of Thessalonica, to serve as his personal vicar. Thus he hoped to
ensure that Rome's influence would not decrease because of
Gratian's political realignment. This vicariate would last
until 732. Later, Pope Zosimus (417–418) would institute a

---

[10] In Migne, *PL*, 13:1131–48, at 1132–33. Translation taken from
Robert Eno, *The Rise of the Papacy* (Wilmington, Del.: Michael Glazier,
1990), 96.

[11] See *Epistola XVII* 7.14, in Migne, *PL*, 20:526–37, at 536.

similar arrangement with the bishop of Arles, eventually
causing difficulties for Leo the Great (440–461), who had to
deal with the complaints against that diocese's bishop,
Hilary.[12] These cases of papal "vicars" should perhaps be
seen less as an exercise of primacy in relation to the church
universal than as an exercise of Rome's authority over the
western half of the empire, which, for a limited period of
time, took this particular form of assigning vicars for Macedonia and for Gaul.[13]

---

[12] See Zosimus, *Epistola I*, in Migne, *PL,* 20:612–15, on the establishment of the vicariate of Arles. For Leo's troubles with Hilary of Arles, see
his tenth letter, addressed to the bishops presiding in the province of
Vienne, in Hunt, *Letters*, 37–47.

[13] So Piepkorn, who writes that Damasus's establishment of a vicar at
Thessalonica "must be seen as a 'patriarchal' rather than a 'papal' action"
("Roman Primacy," 81). In 1922, Pierre Batiffol delivered three conferences at the University of Strasbourg in which he argued that the authority of the bishop of Rome must be seen in relation to three distinct
geographic areas. The area immediately subject to him in about the year
250, to which canon 6 of Nicaea referred when it spoke of the ancient custom acknowledging a wider authority to Alexandria, Antioch, and Rome,
was *Italia suburbicaria*, running from Tuscany (north of Rome including
modern-day Florence) southward to include the rest of the Italian peninsula as well as the islands of Sicily, Sardinia, and Corsica. Within this area
the authority of the Roman bishop was immediate and "quasi monar-
chique"; he participated in the selection and ordination of the other bishops, settled disputes, and watched over the doctrinal, liturgical, and
disciplinary life of the churches. A second zone included the rest of the
western empire beyond suburbicarian Italy: Northern Africa, Spain, the
Gallic territories, and Illyria (Pannonia, Dacia, and Macedonia—the modern Balkan area and Greece). For Batiffol, the Council of Sardica of 343
gave paradigmatic expression to the relation between Rome and the
churches within this area. Most characteristic was its rule that major disciplinary disputes could be appealed to Rome's bishop for review and for
his decision either to allow a local judgment to stand or to reopen the case
to a new local process. Finally, the relation between Rome and the eastern
churches was governed by three principles: recognition of the preeminence
of the faith of Rome, which had succeeded in maintaining correct doctrine
in the face of all of the heresies; the canonical autonomy of the East, such
that the order and disciplinary actions of the eastern churches were han-
dled by the eastern patriarchs; and the necessity for the East to be in com-

Another good example of appeal to the bishop of Rome during the time of Innocent I is the exchange between the bishops of Northern Africa and the pope during the Pelagian controversy. Letters were written from synods held in Carthage and in Milevius which had condemned the teachings of Pelagius and his follower Celestius, asking Innocent to approve their decision "so that likewise the authority of the apostolic see might be added to what has been established by our lesser authority" (*ut statutis nostrae mediocritatis etiam apostolicae sedis adhibeatur auctoritas*).[14] In his reply to the letter of the Synod of Carthage, in which he fully agrees with the doctrinal decisions against Pelagianism, Innocent praises the North African bishops for referring their decision to him, for he occupies the apostolic see, sitting in the place of the apostle [Peter] "from whom the episcopate itself and all authority exercised in his name flows out" (*a quo ipse episcopatus et tota auctoritas nominis hujus emersit*). No decision should be considered final, as assisted by God and not merely of human origin, unless it first comes to the notice of the apostolic see and receives its approval (*Epistola XXIX* 1; Migne, *PL,* 20:583AB). In his response to the bishops of Milevius, Innocent picks up a theme already enunciated by Siricius and borrowed from St. Paul, when he claims that he bears the burden of "solicitude for all the churches" (2 Cor. 11:28). When controversies concerning the faith arise, it is necessary for there to be an arbitrator between all of the

---

munion with the church of Rome, attested to principally by the letters sent upon the election of a new bishop of Alexandria, Antioch, and, later, Constantinople, seeking communion with the Roman bishop. See P. Batiffol, "La 'Potestas' papale. Faits et problèmes de l'histoire des origines de la papauté," part 1 in his *Cathedra Petri* (Paris: Cerf, 1938), 21–79. Piepkorn uses the adjective "patriarchal" for Batiffol's middle zone of authority, a designation that would come into use in the sixth century under the emperor Justinian, according to Batiffol (p. 42).

[14] This phrase is taken from the letter of the council held in Carthage in 416: *Epistola XXVI* 1, in Migne, *PL,* 20:565B. The letter from the synod of Milevius (*Epistola XXVII*) contains a similar request for confirmation from the bishop of Rome.

brother bishops. Who could this be if not Peter (*Epistola XXX* 2; Migne, *PL,* 20:590AB)?

It was this Pelagian episode from the beginning of the fifth century that occasioned the famous Augustinian phrase which was applied to the doctrinal authority of the bishop of Rome: *"causa finita est."* In *Sermo CXXXI* (Migne, *PL,* 38:734), Augustine pointed out that two African synods had condemned the teachings of Pelagius and had sent their decisions to the bishop of Rome, who for his part confirmed the condemnations: "the case is closed." Subsequently the phrase was altered to become *"Roma locuta est, causa finita est,"* which obviously makes no reference whatsoever to the synodal deliberations and request by the bishops for papal agreement, circumstances without which Augustine's statement cannot be adequately understood. The phrase "Rome has spoken" gives the impression that a decision was taken by the bishop of Rome on his own, without any participation by other bishops; nothing could be farther from expressing the true situation at the time of the statement.[15]

Innocent's successor, Zosimus, stumbled for a moment on the Pelagian question, when, in response to a very humble request by Celestius that Zosimus review and correct his doctrine, the pope initially gave it his seal of approval. This occasioned an exchange of letters between him and the African bishops, leading eventually to an unequivocal rejection of Celestius's doctrine by Zosimus (the latter explained to the African bishops that perhaps Celestius had not told him the whole truth), but also to a very strong affirmation that judgments of the bishop of Rome were not open to review by others because of his unique continuation of the ministry of Peter.

> The tradition of the Fathers attributes to the apostolic see such authority that no one would dare to dispute its judgments . . . ; even today reverence is due to the name of Peter

---

[15] See P. Batiffol, "Augustin, Pélage et le siège apostolique (411–417)," in his *Le Catholicisme de S. Augustin,* 2nd ed. (Paris: J. Gabalda, 1920), 349–410, especially 402–10.

... whose power derives from the promise of Christ our God that he might loose what is bound and bind what is loosed; since Peter the head is of such great authority ... the Roman church, in which place we govern, is fortified by divine and human laws ...; although our authority is such that no one can revise our decision [*tamen cum tantum nobis esset auctoritatis, ut nullus de nostra possit retractare sententia*], nevertheless we have taken no action without bringing it to your attention through our letters. (*Epistola XII* 1; Migne, *PL,* 20:676AB)

The claim that no one has the authority to revise the decision of the bishop of Rome is echoed by Zosimus's successor, Boniface (418–422). He associates Bishop Rufus, his vicar in Thessalonica, with the mission of Peter, encouraging him to remain vigilant with the eyes of the blessed apostle Peter, the eternal pastor of the Lord's flocks (*Epistola V* 1; Migne, *PL,* 20:762A). One is never allowed to go back and reconsider a question that has already been determined by the apostolic see (*Nunquam enim licuit de eo rursus, quod semel statutum est ab apostolica sede, tractari* [*Epistola XIII* 2; Migne, *PL,* 20:776A]; see also *Epistola XV* 5; Migne, *PL,* 20:781–82). These statements by Damasus, Siricius, Innocent, Zosimus, and Boniface all associate the bishop of Rome in a unique way with Peter. They insist that Peter's agreement must accompany any final decision within the church and that his judgment cannot be submitted to a higher court of appeal. It is not a long step from these affirmations to the interventions of Popes Celestine (422–432) and Leo I (440–461) at the Councils of Ephesus (431) and Chalcedon (451), nor to the principle that will later play an important role in qualifying the exercise of papal primacy: "the first see is not judged by anyone" (*prima sedes a nemine iudicatur*).

The Bishop of Rome and the Churches of the East

Northern Africa, the Iberian peninsula, Gaul, and Illyricum together formed a great arc encircling the Italian peninsula. They all pertained to the western half of the Roman Empire, as divided by Diocletian and Constantine at the beginning of the fourth century. The letters we have been considering up to this point show that, at the turn of the fifth century, the bishops of these territories acknowledged the unique authority of the bishop of Rome based on the fact that he was the chief pastor of the city where Peter, upon whom Christ founded the church, had exercised his ministry and had given his ultimate witness to Christ unto death. What about the East? Klaus Schatz has pointed out that, of the 179 letters that have survived from popes Damasus to Leo (thus from 384 to 461), ninety-two, or slightly more than half, were exchanges with bishops, clergy, and members of the imperial family, all of whom resided in the East![16] How can this be explained?

First of all, Roman interaction with the East was not an innovation begun by Damasus; we have seen already a few of the previous contacts between the bishops of Rome and the Eastern churches. During the second century there were the discussions over the celebration of Easter at the time of Polycarp and Anicetus (ca. 150) and later when Victor was bishop of Rome (ca. 195). The third century saw the deposition and replacement of Paul of Samosata as bishop of Antioch (ca. 268) and the request by the synod of that church for approval by the bishops of Rome and Alexandria. During the fourth century, Julius I defended Athanasius as the rightful bishop of Alexandria and stood firm in supporting the creed of Nicaea (after 339). The pattern represented by Julius and Athanasius would now be repeated in a series of exchanges between the bishop of Rome and a number of prominent bishops from the East, the first being John Chrysostom.

John was deposed as bishop of Constantinople in 404, not because of any doctrinal controversy but rather because individuals within the ecclesial and imperial establishment

---

[16] K. Schatz, *Papal Primacy: From Its Origins to the Present* (Collegeville, Minn.: Liturgical Press, 1996), 33.

intensely disliked him. Chrysostom, as his epithet indicates, was a persuasive orator who had first served as the cathedral preacher at Antioch before coming to Constantinople. When he was bishop of Constantinople, both his disciplinary actions against wayward clerics and his campaign of reform gained him many enemies, the most powerful of whom was the empress Eudoxia. These enemies eventually conspired with the bishop of Alexandria, Theophilus, to hold a synod in which John was deposed. John appealed to the bishop of Rome, Innocent I, who, finding flaws in the procedure, refused to break communion with him. Innocent wrote several letters both defending John before his enemies and encouraging him after he was exiled. When John died in 407 during a long journey to remove him still further from Constantinople, Innocent broke off communion with Theophilus of Alexandria and his supporters in Constantinople and other Eastern sees, beginning a schism that was not completely healed until Innocent's death ten years later.

Pope Celestine's (422–432) most important contacts with the East also began with an appeal from a bishop. In April of 430, Cyril of Alexandria wrote to elicit Celestine's support against the bishop of Constantinople, Nestorius (see *Epistola XI;* Migne, *PG,* 77:80–89). A synod was held later that year in Rome which, after consulting texts by Ambrose, Damasus, and Hilary of Poitier, approved of the Marian title "Mother of God" (*Theotokos*), which Nestorius had been talked into denying in deference to some of the theologians of the school of Antioch (see Migne, *PL,* 50:457, for the Roman synod's decision). Celestine's letter to Cyril conveys how he understood his contribution as bishop of Rome to the dispute in the East:

> Taking to yourself the authority of our see and acting in our place, you shall carry out this sentence with resolute vigor: that either [Nestorius] shall within ten days . . . condemn by means of a written profession his wicked assertions, and shall affirm that with reference to the birth of Christ our God he will hold the faith which the Roman church, the church of

your holiness, and the Catholic religion holds . . . [or] he is in every way removed from our body.[17]

Thus Celestine delegates to Cyril the authority to act in his name, clearly implying that Celestine's authority was higher than that of Cyril himself. Furthermore, the letter states that Nestorius would be excommunicated within ten days of receiving Celestine's decision should he not recant, a stipulation that would have rendered a subsequent ecumenical council unnecessary. The bishop of Rome evidently believed that the authority of the synod over which he presided in Rome was sufficient to resolve this controversy. Nestorius, however, appealed to the emperor that a council be held, and Pope Celestine went along, so that the third ecumenical council was held the following year (431) in Ephesus. The unfolding of this council is quite complex. Its immediate result was a break between the two major sees of Antioch and Alexandria, which was only resolved two years later in 433 and which led Cardinal Newman, many centuries later, to register disappointment with the tactics of Cyril.[18] But the intervention of the papal representative Philip during the proceedings at Ephesus is quite germane to our theme.

> No one doubts, and indeed it has been known in all ages, that the holy and most blessed Peter, the prince and head of the apostles, the pillar of the faith, the foundation of the Catholic Church . . . even to the present and always lives and judges in his successors. Our holy and most blessed Pope Celestine the bishop is therefore assuredly in due order his successor and lieutenant.[19]

---

[17] In Carl Mirbt and Kurt Aland, *Quellen zur Geschichte des Papsttums und des Römischen Katholizismus*, 6th ed. (Tübingen: Mohr, 1967), §427.

[18] A detailed account of the council can be found in P.-Th. Camelot, *Éphèse et Chalcédoine*, Histoire des conciles 2 (Paris: L'Orante, 1962). Also perhaps the Alberigo text.

[19] In E. Schwartz, *Acta Conciliorum Oecumenicorum*, four tomes, each divided into several volumes (Berlin: de Gruyter, 1914–84), here at

How did the council receive this claim of papal authority? Perhaps this question can be answered by looking at the crucial decision of the council, in which the bishops judged the views of Nestorius to be heretical. They claimed to be led to this judgment after examining Nestorius's teachings and "compelled of necessity both by the canons and by the letter of our most holy father and fellow servant Celestine, bishop of the church of the Romans" (*coacti tam ex canonibus quam ex epistula sanctissimi patris nostri et comministri Caelestini episcopi Romanorum*).[20] Afterwards, they wrote a letter to Celestine, praising his zeal in promoting sound doctrine and his "solicitude for all the churches" (see Migne, *PL,* 50:512–13). Usually these expressions of deference have been interpreted as falling short of a wholesale acceptance of the kind of Roman claim to authority quoted above from the papal legate Philip. The following summary, referring to the Council of Ephesus, seems to reflect the common interpretation of Eastern attitudes toward Rome at the time.

> . . . many historians see in the episode an illustration of a persistent theme in the relations of the churches of the East with the bishop of Rome. The Easterners are willing to accord a kind of primacy to the see of Rome on a political-historical basis. Thus when the Roman see enunciates its claims to universal primacy, the Eastern churches listen and politely refrain from explicitly rejecting these claims, in part at least out of a genuine respect for the see of Peter. The bishops of Rome in turn seem at least at times to have interpreted this Eastern silence as concurrence in the Roman position.[21]

There can be no doubt about the fact that the bishop of Rome played a much more significant role in the actual holding and outcome of the Council of Ephesus than he had in the

---

I/I, iii, 60. Hereafter, this collection will be simply referred to as *ACO,* followed by tome/volume, part, and page numbers.

[20] See Tanner, *Decrees of the Ecumenical Councils,* 1:40–74, at 61–62 for the quoted phrase.

[21] Piepkorn, "Roman Primacy," 90.

earlier two ecumenical councils. Appeal was made to him on
a serious doctrinal question about which major churches of
the East were divided. The decision he made, together with
his Roman synod, was recognized by the ecumenical council
as truly expressing the orthodox faith. There is an explicit
acknowledgment of his authority—the council fathers were
"compelled by the canons and by the letter of their father and
fellow minister Celestine." And yet one cannot dispel the
impression that the conciliar recognition of papal leadership
is more modest than the bold claims made by the bishop of
Rome himself and by his legate at the council.

Leo the Great

With Leo the Great (440–461), both the claim and the exercise of primacy by the bishop of Rome came to the fullest
stage of development that they would reach during the first
millennium.[22] Leo's understanding of his primatial ministry
is nicely conveyed in sermons he delivered on the anniversary of his consecration as bishop of Rome (September 29th)
and on the feast of the apostles Peter and Paul (June 29th).
In two of these (*Sermons 4* and *83*), Leo links together the
three Petrine texts that would become the most common
New Testament passages used by later Catholic theology and
official teaching as supports for papal primacy: Matt.
16:17–19 ("You are Peter and upon this rock I will build my
church"); Luke 22:31–32 ("I have prayed for you that your
faith may not fail and when you have turned again
strengthen your brethren"); and John 21:15–17 ("Simon,
son of John, do you love me? . . . Feed my sheep").[23] The

---

[22] Eno writes: "The pontificate of Leo I has traditionally been viewed
as the high point of the ancient papacy" (*Rise of the Papacy*, 102). He
devotes fifteen pages (pp. 102–17) of his 150-page book to Leo.

[23] The texts of the sermons will be taken from St. Leo the Great, *Ser-
mons*, trans. Jane Patricia Freeland and Agnes Josephine Conway, The
Fathers of the Church 93 (Washington, D.C.: Catholic University of
America Press, 1996). Freeland and Conway follow the same numbering

key to the Roman claim of primacy lay in its assertion of a unique succession of the bishop of Rome to the primatial ministry of the apostle Peter. One hundred years earlier Cyprian of Carthage had acknowledged that all bishops depend on Peter, generally understanding this to mean that each and every bishop was a "successor to Peter."[24] Without denying the truth of Cyprian's insight that all bishops must continue to profess the faith as Peter did in Matthew 16, Leo is nevertheless convinced that the bishop of Rome succeeds Peter in a way that the other bishops do not.

> Peter does not relinquish his government of the Church. . . . So, if we do anything correctly or judge anything correctly, if we obtain anything at all from the mercy of God through daily supplications, it comes about as a result of his works and merits. In this see his power lives on and his authority reigns supreme. . . . Regard him as present in the lowliness of my person. Honor him. In him continues to reside the responsibility for all shepherds, along with the protection of those sheep entrusted to them. His dignity does not fade even in an unworthy heir. (*Sermon 3* §§3–4)[25]

The unique relation of the bishop of Rome to Peter determines his relationship to the other bishops; he is "not only the ruler of this see but the primate of all bishops" (*Sermon 3* §4).

> Although there are many priests and many shepherds among the people of God, it is Peter who properly rules each one of those whom Christ also rules principally. Great and wonder-

---

found in volumes 138 and 138A of Corpus Christianorum Series Latina. Further references to the sermons will be given within parentheses in the text, indicating the sermon and paragraph numbers.

[24] I say "generally" because passages from at least two of his writings, *On the Unity of the Catholic Church* and, especially, *Letter 59*, can be interpreted as acknowledging a unique succession to Peter by the bishop of Rome.

[25] See also *Sermon 3* §2: "For the sturdiness of that faith which was praised in the leader of the apostles endures. Just as what Peter believed in Christ remains, there likewise remains what Christ instituted in Peter."

ful a share of his power did God see fit to bestow upon this man, dearly beloved. If he wanted other leaders to share something with him, whatever he did not refuse entirely to these others he never gave unless it was through him. (*Sermon 4* §2)

Apostles and bishops enjoy a fundamental equality, but one that also admits of "a certain distinction in power."

> For even among the most blessed Apostles, alike in honor, there was a certain distinction in power. Although they were all equal in being chosen, one was allowed to stand out above the others. From this arrangement there arose, also, distinctions among the bishops. And through a vast hierarchy it was provided that everyone might not arrogate everything to himself, but particular bishops were to be set up in each province, whose opinion among the brothers was to be considered first. Certain others, again, were to assume a greater pastoral responsibility in the larger cities. And through them the care of the universal Church was to converge in the one see of Peter, and nothing was ever to be at odds with his leadership. He, therefore, who knows that he has been set above certain others should not take it amiss that another is set over him. But he should also display the same obedience which he demands. And as he himself does not wish to bear the burden of a heavy load, so, too, he should not dare to pile an insupportable load on another. We are disciples of the meek and humble Master, who said: "Learn from me, for I am meek and humble of heart; and you will find rest for your souls. For my yoke is easy, and my burden light" (Matt. 11:29–30). Shall we ever experience this unless still another saying of the Lord finds a place in our observance: "Whoever wishes to become great among you shall be your servant (Matt. 20:26) . . . for whoever exalts himself shall be humbled, and he who humbles himself shall be exalted" (Luke 14:11)?[26]

What is quite remarkable about this text is its simultaneous

---

[26] From *Letter 14* of Leo to Anastasius, bishop of Thessalonica, January 6, 446. Translation taken from Hunt, *Letters*, 66–67.

affirmation of hierarchical order and evangelical humility. That some have a higher authority than others must not for a moment be separated from Jesus' own statements about authority as humble service. This leads Leo to affirm both the equality of and the hierarchical order among bishops. Here it is useful once again to compare Leo with Cyprian. While Cyprian is careful to avoid any statement that might diminish the equality of all the bishops, Leo contends that, on the scale of gospel values, humble service is more important than equality. The hierarchical order of the bishops, converging ultimately "in the one see of Peter," serves the unity of the community throughout the world. Insisting on equality to the detriment of the primatial ministry established in Peter would amount to misunderstanding Jesus' gospel vision of authority as humble service.

This same letter to Anastasius of Thessalonica contains a phrase that would become important for reflection about the primacy of the pope in the West during the second millennium. Leo shares with Anastasius a part of Leo's own "solicitude for all the churches." This expression, from 2 Cor. 11:28, demonstrates that Paul understood his pastoral supervision to extend beyond a single local church. As such, it came to be used frequently by bishops of Rome as a further biblical justification for their supralocal ministry of primacy. Later, the Latin expression *pars sollicitudinis* was employed, often with reference to Leo's letter to Anastasius, to describe the relation between the bishop of Rome and all the other bishops. As we shall see, this idea flourished especially after the distinction between the "power of orders" and the "power of jurisdiction" appeared within canon law in the West toward the end of the twelfth century. Juridically speaking, the pope's "power of jurisdiction" was universal because his "solicitude" extended to all the churches. He would impart a share of this jurisdiction to each bishop on the occasion of his assignment to a particular diocese. Obviously such a conception rendered the local bishop very subordinate to and dependent on the bishop of Rome. It is important to realize that this was clearly not Leo's intention in his letter to Anastasius. Anastasius was the bishop of Thessalonica, precisely that see whose chief pastor had been designated as "vicar" to the bishop of Rome since the time of Damasus.[27] The "sharing of solicitude" about which Leo here speaks must be understood within that context, not as a statement about the relation between the bishop of Rome and all other bishops.

Letter 10, written to the bishops of the province of Vienne, provides some fascinating information about Leo's difficult relations with another vicar, this time in the vicariate of Arles which Zosimus had set up in 417. Its bishop, Hilary, had usurped some of the rightful tasks of the metropolitan bishops of Gaul. In his letter, Leo not only corrects Hilary and restricts his authority henceforth to his own diocese, but also takes the opportunity to comment on the Petrine ministry in relation to the bishops throughout the world. It is precisely because God willed that the message of the gospel go out to the ends of the earth (see Ps. 18:5) that Peter was given a unique role among the apostles.

> Now, the Lord desired that the dispensing of this gift [the proclamation of the gospel] should be shared as a task by all the Apostles, but in such a way that He put the principal charge on the most blessed Peter, the highest of all the Apostles. He wanted His gifts to flow into the entire body from Peter himself, as it were from the head. Thus, a man who had dared to separate himself from the solidity of Peter would realize that he no longer shared in the divine mystery. The Lord wanted Peter . . . to be named from what he really was [the rock] . . . so that the building of the eternal temple . . . might stand on the solidity of Peter.[28]

---

[27] J. Macdonald argues that the formal establishment of this vicariate goes back not to Damasus (366–384) but to Innocent I (401–417) ("Who Instituted the Papal Vicariate of Thessalonica?" in *Studia Patristica*, vol. 4, ed. F. L. Cross [Berlin: Akademie-Verlag, 1961], 478–82).

[28] Hunt, *Letters*, 37.

For Leo, just as the unifying and solidifying role of Peter did not detract from the dignity of the other apostles, so too the role of the bishop of Rome does not diminish the other bishops: "For our solicitude, which seeks not its own interests but those of Christ, does not detract from the dignity given by God to the churches and the bishops of the churches. This was the procedure always well observed and profitably maintained by our predecessors. But Hilary has departed from it. . . ."[29]

The Council of Chalcedon

Early in 448, at what turned out to be approximately the midpoint of his pontificate, Leo received a letter from one whom he called in his reply of June 1, 448, a "dearly beloved son," the abbot Eutyches of Constantinople. Eutyches had written to warn Leo of a new outbreak of the "heinous poison" of Nestorianism. Later in November of that year, Flavian, the bishop of Constantinople, condemned this same Eutyches for spreading his own heretical poison. From this point on, many of the 150 letters that Leo either wrote or received until his death in 461 are concerned with the Eutyches affair and the various events that stemmed from it: the "robber council" of Ephesus (449), the fourth ecumenical council of Chalcedon (451), the disapproval of the twenty-eighth canon of Chalcedon and the struggle between monophysites and Chalcedonians over the see of Alexandria.

After several further letters of clarification from Eutyches, Flavian, and the emperor Theodosius II, Leo wrote his famous twenty-eighth letter—the "tome to Flavian"—dated June 13, 449. This tome gathered and commented on many biblical texts in such a way as to set forth the orthodox doctrine of the incarnation which faithfully had been handed on by the previous ecumenical councils. By clearly affirming both the divinity and humanity of Christ, it justified

---

[29] Ibid., 38–39.

Flavian's condemnation of Eutyches, who had proposed a "one nature" model for the incarnation. Leo's tome was undoubtedly the most important doctrinal statement by a bishop of Rome up until that time and arguably the most significant papal pronouncement ever made.

In the meantime, a group of Eutyches' supporters, including his nephew, the eunuch Chrysaphius, convinced the emperor Theodosius to convoke a council at Ephesus in August of 449 for the purpose of rehabilitating Eutyches, deposing Flavian, and opposing the Nestorians. The bishop of Rome was also invited and sent three legates to this council. Theodosius set up as president of the council Dioscorus, the bishop of Alexandria, who opposed any doctrine even remotely related to Nestorianism, which had originated in Alexandria's theological rival Antioch, including, as it turned out, the orthodox teaching that the divine and human natures were united in the incarnation of the Word of God. Flavian and his supporters were not allowed to speak during the proceedings and Dioscorus put off the requests of the Roman legates to read Leo's tome. In the end, Flavian was condemned and deposed; he died shortly thereafter on his way into exile. Other bishops suspected of Nestorianism were also dismissed—Theodoret of Cyr, Ibas of Edessa, and Domnus of Antioch. The tremendous significance of these events lay in the fact that Ephesus attempted to be an ecumenical council, all the while reducing to silence and condemning bishops from important Eastern sees and, most of all, excluding the doctrinal contribution and agreement of the bishop of Rome. Leo's *Letter 95* (July 20, 451) to the new empress Pulcheria, who with her husband Marcian succeeded to the throne after the death of Theodosius II, called it "that robbery (*latrocinium*) at Ephesus; it was not a council."

A new council, opened at Nicaea in 451 but soon transferred to Chalcedon, where the emperor Marcian could keep a closer watch on it, reversed the decisions of the robber synod of Ephesus. Leo's tome was read and accepted to the exclamation of the bishops: "Peter has spoken through Leo"

(*ACO* II/I, ii, 81 [277]). The Roman representative Lucentius condemned Dioscorus for presuming unlawfully to hold a synod without the consent of the bishop of Rome (*ACO* II/I, i, 65). Dioscorus was replaced in Alexandria with a bishop who followed the teaching of Chalcedon, Proterius, although he was to be assassinated six years later and replaced by the monophysite (one nature) bishop Timothy Aelurus. Leo's final letters are mostly devoted to trying to return a Chalcedonian bishop to Alexandria. While Flavian, Theodoret, Ibas, and Domnus were all exonerated, the fifth ecumenical council, II Constantinople, almost exactly one hundred years later (553), condemned several writings of Theodoret and Ibas, thus showing that the christological debate continued to stir up controversy for many decades. Because of all the intrigue that surrounded the Council of Chalcedon, Leo began the long-standing practice by which the bishop of Rome maintained a representative, with the title of *apocrisiarius*, at the imperial court in Constantinople.

At the close of the council, the assembled bishops wrote to Leo, recounting what had taken place and asking him "to accept our definition . . . as though it were your own." Perhaps with the intention to hasten that acceptance, they wrote rather fawningly:

> You have indeed preserved the faith, which has come down to us like a golden stream in the command of our divine Teacher. Constituted, as you are, the interpreter of the words of blessed Peter for all mankind, you have poured forth upon the universe the blessings he elicited by his faith. Hence we have looked to you as the leader of our religion to our great advantage. And we have demonstrated for the children of the Church the lineage and strength of the faith, not separately and singly declaring its teachings in secret, but with one heart, together in peace, making profession of our belief.[30]

---

[30] Text in Schwartz, *ACO* II/I, 475–77. This translation is taken from F. X. Murphy, *Peter Speaks through Leo: The Council of Chalcedon A.D. 451* (Washington, D.C.: Catholic University of America Press, 1952), 95–96.

The recognition of Leo as interpreter of Peter "for all mankind" is quite significant in light of the effort by the bishops of Rome to emphasize precisely that point ever since their surprise at the third canon of I Constantinople. Still the letter from Chalcedon did not hide the fact that it too was seeking Leo's agreement to a canon which his representatives had resisted. It was canon 28.

Canon 28 reaffirmed I Constantinople's objectional third canon in a much more elaborate text, the principal sentence of which read as follows:

> The fathers [of I Constantinople] rightly accorded prerogatives to the see of older Rome, since that is an imperial city; and moved by the same purpose the new Rome, reasonably judging that the city which is honoured by the imperial power and senate and enjoying privileges equalling older imperial Rome, should also be elevated to her level in ecclesiastical affairs and take second place after her.[31]

The rationale for acknowledging a special prerogative of Rome or of any other city was exclusively its relation to "the imperial power and senate." It is not hard to imagine how Leo would react to such a canon. In *Letter 104*, addressed to the emperor Marcian in May of 452, he alleges that the conciliar approval of this canon was orchestrated by the bishop of Constantinople, Anatolius, for motives of personal ambition. Nothing may alter the canons of Nicaea, which spoke of the precedence of the three sees of Alexandria, Rome, and Antioch. Leo adds:

> As is our wish, let the city of Constantinople have its glory and under the protecting hand of God, may it long enjoy your Clemency's rule. Nevertheless, things secular and things religious do not have the same basis; nothing erected is going to be stable apart from that rock which the Lord placed in the foundation. He who hankers after what is not his due loses what is his own. Let it suffice for the man mentioned [Anatolius] to have obtained the bishopric of so great a city

---

[31] Tanner, *Decrees of the Ecumenical Councils*, 1:100.

through your Piety's assistance and my favoring consent. Let
him not disdain the emperor's city though he cannot make it
into the Apostolic See, and let him not hope in any way to
aggrandize himself through injuries done to others.[32]

The key to Leo's response is the conviction that merely secular considerations cannot serve as the basis for ecclesial
order, at least in matters that derive from God's will for the
church. The rock to which Leo refers in this letter is obviously Peter, and it is the Lord himself who placed this rock
"in the foundation." It is beyond the authority of any human
being to make the church of any particular city into the
"apostolic see." Leo eventually agreed to the work accom-
plished by Chalcedon (*Letter 114* of March 21, 453), with
the proviso, however, that he did not and would never accept
canon 28.

Was it ever accepted by the bishop of Rome? The 21st
canon of IV Constantinople (869–870), which the Roman
church considers to be the eighth ecumenical council but
which was never accepted as such by the East, speaks about
the honor due to "all those who hold the office of patriarch," adding: "This applies in the first place to the most
holy pope of old Rome, secondly to the patriarch of
Constantinople, and then to the patriarchs of Alexandria,
Antioch and Jerusalem."[33] No reference to the political
motivation of this ranking is contained in this canon. Later,
the Fourth Lateran Council (1215), held under Pope Innocent III, speaks of the dignity of the patriarchs in its fifth
canon. Here a "primacy of ordinary power" over all other
churches is attributed to the church of Rome, based on "the
Lord's disposition." After Rome, the first place is attributed
to Constantinople, followed by Alexandria, Antioch, and
Jerusalem.[34] Thus the ranking of the five sees would appear

---

[32] Hunt, *Letters*, 179.
[33] Tanner, *Decrees of the Ecumenical Councils*, 1:182.
[34] Ibid., 1:236.

to be fully accepted by the West, but not canon 28's mere political rationale for the ranking.

Summary:
Ubi Petrus ibi ecclesia
(Ambrose, Enarrationes in 12 Psalmos Davidicos 40.30)

Some have argued that it is only by looking at the period after the official toleration of Christianity by the Roman Empire and after the holding of the first ecumenical councils that one can begin to understand the relation between primacy and episcopacy in a way that truly respects the historical development of each.[35] It seems true that a certain degree of worldwide self-awareness on the part of the church is necessary before this relationship can come into focus. The very writing of Eusebius's history at the beginning of the fourth century witnesses to the fact that the church had begun to enjoy such a more global outlook after the edict of toleration finally had ended the persecutions. At first, the emperor was the only obvious authoritative figure on this wider stage.[36] But Constantine, not yet himself even baptized, realized the need for a properly ecclesial organ that could act with the authority needed to maintain unity throughout the whole catholic world. By convoking the first ecumenical council, Constantine obviously was not creating

---

[35] Recently this point is made by Stefan Horn, "Das Verhältnis von Primat und Episkopat im ersten Jahrtausend: Eine geschichtlich-theologische Synthese," in *Il primato del successore di Pietro*, Atti e Documenti 7 (Vatican City: Libreria Editrice Vaticana, 1998), 194–213, at 194–95.

[36] Horn ("Das Verhältnis von Primat und Episkopat," 203–10) and others argue that one cannot begin to grasp the relation between primacy and episcopacy during the period after the edict of toleration without being attentive also to the role of the emperor. For Horn, the struggle over the ranking of Constantinople is not primarily a struggle between the bishop of Rome and the eastern bishops but rather between the pope and the emperor, whose considerable authority and geographical proximity the Eastern bishops had to respect.

ex nihilo the synodal structure of the church, the roots of
which go back to the New Testament and the actualization
of which had already found many regional expressions during the second and third centuries. Moreover, the very first
ecumenical council also recognized a supralocal and personal (as distinct from synodal) authority, already established by "ancient custom," in the sees of Alexandria,
Rome, and Antioch. When the second ecumenical council
attempted to add the city of Constantinople to this group,
ranking it after Rome and before Alexandria and Antioch
because it was now the capital of the empire, the Roman
bishop, often quite understandably supported by the bishop
of Alexandria, objected.[37] A unique relation with Peter,
upon whom Jesus promised to found his church, was the
only sustainable motive for primatial authority within the
Christian community.

Of the Petrine sees mentioned by the sixth canon of
Nicaea, Rome unquestionably held the highest place, not
only because there Peter was martyred and buried but also
because Rome had fared better in preserving the orthodox
faith. No doubt because they were lively centers of theological thought and writing, both Alexandria and Antioch had,
at one time or another, given birth to heretical teachings and
been shepherded by bishops who were tainted with such
doctrines. Of bishops who could in a special way claim to
succeed to Peter, the bishop of Rome indisputably held the
first place.

Thus, no other city laid claim to a primacy within the
entire Christian community on the basis of its relation to
Peter. It seems accurate to say that, to some extent, the other
churches accepted Rome's claim. Of course the all-important

---

[37] When the emperor Theodosius I made it the official religion of the
empire in *Cunctos popolos* of February 27, 380, he defined Christianity
as the religion which Peter the apostle had handed on to the Romans and
which, at the present time, was followed by Bishops Damasus of Rome
and Peter of Alexandria. Text in C. Kirch, *Enchiridion Fontium Historiae
Ecclesiasticae Antiquae* (Barcelona: Herder, 1960), nos. 828, 471–72.

phrase here is "to some extent." For example, the Council of
Sardica (343) spoke of the right to appeal major cases to
Rome, out of deference to Peter. There are many instances of
such appeal to the bishop of Rome during the fourth and
fifth centuries. In the West, appeals concerned not only
major doctrinal questions, such as the request for the agreement sought by the North African synods about Pelagianism, but also disciplinary issues, such as those covered in the
first papal decretal sent by Siricius to Spain or in the numerous directives issued to the vicars in Thessalonica. The East
also appealed to the bishop of Rome; one thinks immediately of the letters written by Athanasius, Basil of Caesarea,
John Chrysostom, Cyril of Alexandria, Eutyches, Flavian,
and Theodoret.[38] At times these appeals concerned doctrine,
in which cases the decision of Rome's bishop inevitably won
the acceptance of the other bishops. When it came to personal appeals by bishops or clergy who felt they had been
deposed unjustly, Rome's decision was not always accepted.
The immediate response to Innocent I's support of John
Chrysostom is a good example of such nonreception on the
part of the East. In the West, there is the famous case of
ousted cleric Apiarius, an African who had sought to be reinstated by appealing to the pope. After several heated
exchanges, a council of Carthage sternly forbid any further
recourse to Rome "across the sea" and chided the pope with
a letter that Robert Eno calls "one of the most angry ever
written to Rome."[39]

With regard to the relation between the bishop of Rome

---

[38] The present chapter has mentioned all of these except Basil, whose
seventieth letter, from the year 371, is usually understood as urging Pope
Damasus (366–384) to intervene against the progress of Arianism in the
East; so J. Quasten, *Patrology* (Westminster: Newman Press, 1960),
3:206. See also P. Batiffol, "Les recours à Rome en Orient avant le concile
de Chalcédoine," in *Cathedra Petri*, 215–48, who gives many other examples of Eastern appeals to Rome.

[39] Eno, *Rise of the Papacy*, 77, for this comment, and pp. 75–79 for
the whole course of events.

and the ecumenical councils, it is clear that papal interventions were invariably occasioned by a divided episcopate. This is surely the case both in the arduous fifty-year process that culminated when I Constantinople definitively accepted Nicene orthodoxy as well as in the Roman contributions to Ephesus and Chalcedon. This pattern would reappear later at the time of the sixth and seventh ecumenical councils (III Constantinople in 680–681 and II Nicaea in 787). In every case, it was not as if the bishop of Rome stood over against the other bishops, but rather, standing in their midst and responding to their request, he sought to exercise his Petrine responsibility to promote unity. The experience of rival councils promulgating opposing doctrines led Celestine and Leo to insist that the Councils of Ephesus and Chalcedon not treat their papal interventions as "open for further discussion." And yet Leo's tome was not an arbitrary pronouncement issued from on high but an effort to draw upon scripture and tradition in such a way that the bishops might be able readily to receive his teaching as the authentic expression of the faith. The heterodoxy of the robber synod of Ephesus demonstrated the general principle advanced by the popes that only in union with Rome can the decision of an ecumenical council be valid; without or against the successor to Peter a conciliar decision cannot hope to be final. Thus it is not inaccurate to conclude that Roman leadership was truly primatial, with an awareness of a duty and an authority to lead, but at the same time carried out in reference to the college as a whole and usually in a synodal way.[40]

---

[40] J. Lécuyer gathers examples from each of the popes of the 400s which show their respect for the dignity and unity of the body of bishops as a whole ("Collégialité Épiscopale selon les papes du Vᵉ siècle," in *La collegialité episcopale,* Unam sanctam 52 [Paris: Cerf, 1965], 41–57). Within the college of bishops, the pope occupies the place that Peter had held in the body of the Twelve. Often the popes see this role as that of the "head of the body," a conception that, according to Yves Congar, would not have been accepted by the East (see *Ministeri et comunione ecclesiale* [Bologna: Edizioni Dehoniane, 1973], 83-104).

CHAPTER 4

Gregory the Great Looks North: Entering the Middle Ages

In the early sixteenth century, the great Renaissance artist Raphael painted a magnificent fresco on the wall of the Vatican apartment of Leo X, depicting the latter's famous predecessor, Leo the Great, in the act of withstanding Attila the Hun before the gates of Rome. In fact, the reason that the earlier Leo had given for not attending the Council of Chalcedon in 451 was that he was too occupied with caring for the needs of his people in the face of the barbarian threat. Imperial power in the West already had declined substantially by this time, and the "fall of the Roman Empire"—meaning, of course, its western half, in which the city of Rome was located—is usually dated from the deposition of the puppet emperor Romulus Augustulus by Odoacer in 476, only fifteen years after Leo's death. Great social changes were afoot. Although Justinian (emperor, 527-565) would attempt to reestablish the glory of the old empire, causing Rome to be placed under the civil authority of the East once again until Pope Zachary (741–752), of Greek origin, finally allied himself with the Franks two centuries later, for the time being Rome and its bishops were somewhat independent from Constantinople.

The Acacian Schism, Pope Gelasius, and the Formula of Hormisdas

This perhaps helps to explain the boldness of the Roman response to the attempt by Acacius (471–489), the patriarch of Constantinople, to heal the divisions that still remained with the monophysites, especially the patriarch of Alexandria, Peter Mongos (477–490), who had never accepted Chalcedon. Acacius was under pressure from the Eastern emperor Zeno (474–491), who issued the *Henoticon* in 482, a text that condemned both Nestorius and Eutyches and affirmed the creed of Nicaea and the twelve anathemas of Cyril but refrained from using the precise language of Chalcedon: that the incarnation is to be understood in terms of the unity of two natures in one person. To Pope Simplicius (468–483) this seemed nothing less than an attempt to tamper with the definition of the fourth ecumenical council, seeking reconciliation with the heretical monophysites by watering down the orthodox doctrine of both Chalcedon and Leo. Simplicius's fifth and sixth letters state that Peter himself was the source of Leo's contribution to Chalcedon; his teaching may not be revised.[1] The problem of determining whether and how the doctrinal decision of Chalcedon might be further nuanced would dominate the next two ecumenical councils, which punctuated the following two centuries (II Constantinople in 553 and III Constantinople in 680–681). Even after the deaths of Acacius and Zeno, a schism with Rome continued because the Roman bishops insisted that Acacius be explicitly repudiated by the East, which the Eastern bishops were unwilling to do, partly out of resistance to the idea that the bishop of Rome could, on his own and without the agreement of a council or of the other patriarchs, depose the patriarch of Constantinople.[2]

The papal split with the East continued under Simplicius's successors, especially Gelasius I (492–496). Gelasius is one of the most outspoken popes of the first millennium in claiming authority for himself as Peter's successor. He seems

---

[1] Migne, *PL*, 58:35–62.

[2] See W. H. C. Frend, "Eastern Attitudes to Rome during the Acacian Schism," in *The Orthodox Churches and the West*, Studies in Church History 13 (Oxford: Blackwell, 1976), 69–82.

to be the first to have been called the "vicar of Christ"—and that six times—by the Roman synod of 495.[3] Writing to Faustus, his representative in Constantinople, he speaks of Rome's role as final arbiter within the church:

> The canons themselves willed the appeals of the whole Church to be referred to the examination of this see. From it, they also decreed that no appeal whatever ought to be made, and thereby that it should judge the whole Church and come under the judgment of no one. (*Epistola 10* §5)[4]

Apparently Gelasius here is referring to the canons of Sardica (343), which stipulated this right of appeal to Rome out of deference to Peter and which Gelasius, not unlike several of his predecessors, wrongly assigns to the Council of Nicaea (*Epistola 12* §9). The statement about not coming under the judgment of others appears to be one of the earliest forms of what later would become an important principle about the primacy: *prima sedes a nemine iudicatur* ("the first see is judged by no one").[5] This principle finds even stronger expression in *Epistola 26* §5:

> The see of blessed Peter the Apostle has the right to unbind what has been bound by sentences of any pontiffs whatsoever, in that it has the right of judging the whole Church. Neither is it lawful for anyone to judge its judgment, seeing that the canons have willed that it may be appealed to from any part of the world, but that no one may be allowed to appeal from it.[6]

The succinct phrasing of this principle—"the first see is

---

[3] See Migne, *PL* 59: 190C. Note 8 of this edition gives the variant reading that Gelasius was hailed as Christ's vicar eleven (xi) times, instead of six (vi).

[4] Text in A. Thiel, *Epistolae romanorum pontificium genuinae et quae ad eos scriptae sunt . . .* , vol. 1 (Brunsbergae: E. Peter, 1868), 344.

[5] See S. Vacca, *Prima sedes a nemine iudicatur: Genesi e sviluppo storico dell'assioma fino al decreto di Graziano*, Miscellanea Historiae Pontificiae 61 (Rome: Editrice Pontificia Università Gregoriana, 1993).

[6] In Thiel, *Epistolae,* 399–400.

judged by no one"—appears shortly after Gelasius, when it was used to defend Pope Symmachus (498–514) from a threatened deposition by a Roman synod. It later acquired a secular application under Charlemagne, who opened an investigation into complaints against Pope Leo III (795–816), at which it was concluded that the pope could not be judged or sentenced by any earthly court, including that of the emperor.[7] Clearly the *prima sedes* principle goes beyond the canons of Sardica, which merely granted a defendant in major cases (*causae maiores*) the right to appeal to the pope, who, in turn, could judge that a second trial be carried out locally. The principle reveals one of the inherent and perhaps inescapable paradoxes about primatial ministry as such. On the one hand, it is logically consistent that, for the primacy to be able to carry out its specific role of bringing peace and unity to the community when a crisis so requires, then the primate must have sufficient authority that his decision will be accepted by the church as a whole, thus preserving the community from endless vacillation or doctrinal revision. On the other hand, every minister stands under the authority and Word of God. The traditionally acknowledged possibility that a pope could fall into heresy suggests that, while in theory the *prima sedes* principle is consistent, in practice it must allow room for dealing with a serious doctrinal failure on the part of the primatial minister.

Gelasius enunciated one further principle, now concerning church–state relations, which was partially anticipated more than century earlier, when St. Ambrose of Milan corrected the emperor for meddling in the doctrinal controversies of the church. It may be called the "two-powers" theory. Gelasius writes to the emperor Anastasius:

> I beg your Piety not to judge duty to divine truth as arrogance. I hope that it will not have to be said of a Roman

---

[7] So K. Schatz, *Papal Primacy: From Its Origins to the Present* (Collegeville, Minn.: Liturgical Press, 1996), 73.

emperor that he resented the truth being brought home to him. There are indeed, most august emperor, two powers by which this world is chiefly ruled: the sacred authority of the Popes and the royal power. Of these, the priestly power is much more important, because it has to render an account for the kings of men themselves at the divine tribunal. For you know, our very clement son, that although you have the chief place in dignity over the human race, yet you must submit yourself faithfully to those who have charge of divine things and look to them for the means of your salvation. (*Epistola 12* §2)[8]

Medieval theologians later wrote of the "two swords" which Jesus and the disciples carried to the garden of Gethsemane (see Luke 22:38) as representing the power of the keys entrusted by Jesus to the church (*sacerdotium* or *ecclesia*) and the power of secular rulers to govern on behalf of the good of society (*regnum* or *imperium*).[9] Since the power of secular rulers often affected relations between the pope and the other bishops, this principle would have far-reaching consequences upon that relation.

The Acacian schism ended in 519 after a new emperor, Justin I (518–527) renounced the *Henoticon* and sought to reestablish unity with Rome. Pope Hormisdas (514–523) drew up a *libellus* that was signed by the emperor, the patriarch of Constantinople and some two hundred other Eastern bishops and which affirmed not only the doctrine of Chalcedon but also the fact that Jesus' promise that the gates of hell would not prevail against the church founded on Peter (Matt. 16:18) had, in fact, been historically verified in the apostolic see (Rome), "where the Catholic religion has been preserved without stain" and where is to be found "the

---

[8] Text in Thiel, *Epistolae*, 350–51.

[9] See Angel Antón, "La doctrina eclesiastica de las 'Dos Espadas' y de la 'Plenitudo potestatis' en el Papa," in *El Misterio de la Iglesia* (Madrid: BAC, 1986), 1:119–55.

whole, true and perfect solidity of the Christian religion."[10]
The "Formula of Hormisdas" was one of the strongest
acknowledgments of the authority of the bishop of Rome
ever accepted by the East.

The steady growth of self-confident claims to authority on
the part of the bishops of Rome, which had begun immediately after I Constantinople with Damasus, underwent a
humiliating setback during the pontificate of Pope Vigilius
(537–555). Still trying to reconcile the remaining enemies to
Chalcedon in the East, the emperor Justinian supported a
plan to condemn parts of the writings of three deceased
theologians whom the monophysites found particularly
offensive: Theodore of Mopsuestia (d. 428, the teacher of
Nestorius), Theodoret of Cyrrhus (d. 466, who had written
some sharply critical works against Cyril of Alexandria) and
Ibas of Edessa (d. 457, who had written a letter also highly
critical of Cyril to the Persian bishop Maris). Justinian's
efforts ultimately led to the holding of the fifth ecumenical
council (II Constantinople) in 553, whose major outcome
was the condemnation of the "Three Chapters," or lists, of
the objectionable writings of the three authors mentioned.
Vigilius at first opposed such a condemnation on the grounds
that at least two of those to be condemned, Theodoret and
Ibas, were approved by Chalcedon. To condemn them
seemed to submit the decisions of that council once again to
further revision. After being taken to Constantinople by Justinian, Vigilius was pressured eventually to acquiesce in the
council's decision, and he died during his return voyage to
Rome. This time it was the West that had trouble with the
action of the Roman bishop. They saw Vigilius as repudiat-

---

[10] *Enchiridion symbolorum, definitionum et declarationum de rebus
fidei et morum*, ed. H. Denzinger, rev. P. Hünermann, 37th ed. (Freiburg:
Herder, 1991), nos. 171–72 (hereafter DH). The paragraph numbers,
before the new material added by Hünermann, correspond to those of the
36th edition by A. Schönmetzer, usually referred to with the abbreviation
DS.

ing Leo and Chalcedon. The pope's prestige fell in Africa and
Spain, and the ecclesial provinces of Milan and Aquileia
actually broke off communion with Rome for several
decades.

Gregory the Great

Vigilius's successors, especially Pelagius I (556–561) and
Pelagius II (579–590), adopted a more humble style in their
correspondence with the other bishops, insisting on their own
fidelity to Chalcedon and even inviting other bishops to send
delegates to Rome to verify their own orthodoxy. Pelagius II's
third letter to the bishops of Istria is a long, step-by-step
defense of the actions taken by Vigilius and II Constantinople.[11] It argues that Chalcedon's definition does not require
the church to approve all of the writings of the council's par-
ticipants. The future Pope Gregory I, recently returned from
Constantinople, where he had served as Pelagius II's *apocrisiarius*, was the author of this detailed defense.[12] Even when
he became pope, Gregory too found it necessary to protest his
own orthodoxy, which occasioned the famous letter to Savi-
nus, the subdeacon (592 or 593), in which he compared the
first four ecumenical councils to the four Gospels.

> Bad men have gone forth and disturbed your minds, under-
> standing neither what they say nor whereof they affirm, pre-
> tending that in the times of Justinian of pious memory
> something was detracted from the faith of the synod of Chal-
> cedon, which with all faith and all devotion we venerate. And
> in like manner all the four synods of the holy universal
> Church we receive as we do the four books of the holy
> Gospel.[13]

---

[11] It can be found in *ACO* IV, 2, 105–36, which includes all three letters to the bishops of Istria; also available among the letters from and to
Pelagius II in Migne, *PL,* 72:703–90.

[12] So Robert Eno, *The Rise of the Papacy* (Wilmington, Del.: Michael
Glazier, 1990), 140.

[13] *Letter 3* §10. English from *A Select Library of the Nicene and Post-*

Interestingly enough, he refers to *four* synods (Nicaea, I Constantinople, Ephesus, and Chalcedon). Obviously Gregory did not consider the troublesome II Constantinople on the same level as the earlier councils.

Gregory the Great is the other major theologian-pope of the first millennium; of all the bishops of Rome, only he and his predecessor Leo have been given the epithet "the Great." His writings include a treatise on pastoral care which frankly admits the sacrifices required of one who assumes the burden of being pastor. Gregory evidently missed the freedom he had enjoyed as a monk. He goes on to discuss the life of virtue and humility necessary for ministry and gives advice about adapting preaching to the situation of one's listeners. His sense of being a pastor led Gregory to initiate the mission to England and to maintain close ties with the church there. Beginning in 601, the Anglo-Saxon metropolitans of Canterbury and York received the pallium, the symbol of their ministry as metropolitans, from the pope. Gregory encouraged Augustine of Canterbury, the leader of the mission, to make use of whatever liturgical customs from any part of the church that seemed to him advantageous for responding to the sensibilities of the people. Augustine was also to build upon the indigenous culture, adopting its values and integrating them into the life of the church. Thus, Gregory initiates and exemplifies another possible dimension of primatial ministry: promoting the evangelical outreach of the church *ad gentes*. This role by the primate in promoting the church's "foreign missions" would continue in later centuries and would seem to justify at times a dominant role of the primate in providing bishops for young churches. This once again has an obvious effect on the relation between the pope and the bishops.

Finally, Gregory was very sensitive to the fact that the primatial role for one bishop could be misconstrued or misused

Nicene Fathers, Second Series, vol. 12 (Grand Rapids: Eerdmans, 1979), part 2, p. 127.

so as to diminish the honor due to the others. Unlike some of his predecessors, he strongly criticized the title "universal bishop" because "if one is the universal bishop, then the rest of you are not bishops."[14] In a letter of fraternal correction to Bishop Natalis he wrote: "I do myself an injury if I disturb the rights of my brothers."[15] Because of this, Gregory was a popular source for those bishops of Vatican I who feared that the definition of papal primacy would diminish the dignity and responsibility that properly belonged to each bishop.[16] In the end, the third chapter of *Pastor aeternus* was revised to include some sentences from Gregory: "My honour is the honour of the whole church. My honour is the steadfast strength of my brethren. Then do I receive true honour, when it is denied to none of those to whom honour is due."[17]

After Gregory, the principal event of the seventh century relevant to the primacy was the controversy over monothelitism—the teaching that in Christ there was only one will, the divine will. This constituted yet another attempt to achieve full communion with the monophysites. Unfortunately, it implied a denial of the human will of Jesus, and thus a denial of his full humanity. In the early phase of the

---

[14] *Letter IX* §68; translation from *The Nicene and Post-Nicene Fathers*, Second Series, vol. 13 (Grand Rapids: Eerdmans, 1979), 19. In this letter to Bishop Eusebius of Thessalonica, Gregory is objecting to the effort of Patriarch John of Constantinople to apply to himself the adjective "ecumenical," which Gregory takes as meaning "universal." But so absolute is the affirmation that Gregory surely would apply the same principle to himself.

[15] *Letter II* §52; translation from *Nicene and Post-Nicene Fathers*, 13:119.

[16] See Mansi 52, col. 574 (= Doupanloup of June 16, 1870, citing Gregory's letters *IX* §68; *XI* §37; and *II* §52); col. 393 (= Strossmayer of June 2, 1870, citing letters to the emperor Mauritius and to the bishops Eulogius and Anastasius); and col. 666 (= Haynald, citing the letter to Eulogius VIII,30).

[17] Norman P. Tanner, ed., *Decrees of the Ecumenical Councils* (Washington, D.C.: Georgetown University Press, 1990), 2:814.

exploration of this latest attempt to win over the anti-Chalcedonians, Pope Honorius I (625–638) had written to Patriarch Sergius of Constantinople, stating that he could see a kind of sense in the monothelite proposal.[18] After his death, however, the Lateran synod held by Pope Martin I (649–653) in 649 condemned it, thus also winning praise from opponents of monothelitism such as Maximus the Confessor, who acknowledged the Roman church as a standard for orthodox faith and communion.[19] The actual Roman contribution to the sixth ecumenical council (III Constantinople) of 680-681 was fashioned during a synod held under Pope Agatho at Easter of 680 and was mentioned in the ecumenical council's definition of faith.

> This same holy and universal synod, here present, faithfully accepts and welcomes with open hands the report of Agatho, most holy and most blessed pope of elder Rome, that came to our most reverend and most faithful emperor Constantine, which rejected by name those who proclaimed and taught, as has been already explained, one will and one principle of action in the incarnate dispensation of Christ our true God.[20]

In the same paragraph, III Constantinople goes on to recall Leo's earlier contribution in 451 to Chalcedon.[21] But such recognition of the doctrinal leadership of these Roman bishops is counterbalanced by the explicit condemnation of the error of Pope Honorius I, a fact that would make his case a hot topic of discussion during the infallibility debate at Vatican I. Most scholars today would agree that, while Honorius clearly erred in supporting monothelitism, his sup-

---

[18] Schatz, *Papal Primacy*, 54: "Pope Honorius I (625–638) accepted such a formula in 634 in his letters to Patriarch Sergius of Constantinople, or at least he claimed to see some sense in it."

[19] *PG*, 91:137–38; Mansi 10:691–92.

[20] Original text and this translation can be found in Tanner, *Decrees of the Ecumenical Councils*, 1:126.

[21] See P. Conte, "Il significato del primato papale nei padri del VI concilio ecumenico," *Archivum Historiae Pontificiae* 15 (1977): 7–111.

port hardly amounts to a solemn definition. Thus, his case cannot serve as a contradiction of Vatican I, which carefully limited its statement about infallibility to those particularly solemn moments when a bishop of Rome intends to teach "*ex cathedra.*"

The New Ecclesial Geography of the 700s

The dawn of the eighth century revealed a strikingly new ecclesiastical map. The expansion of Islam, from around 650 on, had swallowed up Egypt and Syria, precisely the areas that had been the strongholds of the monophysites. The monothelite doctrine had been devised in the hope of enticing just these Christians back into unity with the Chalcedonians. Now that whole effort had been made for the time being at least practically irrelevant because of the Muslim advances. In 697 Carthage, which for nearly five hundred years had been the great ecclesiastical center of North Africa, was conquered by the Arabs and, fourteen years later, with the defeat of the Visigoths in 711, most of the Iberian peninsula rapidly fell into Muslim hands. Of all the churches in the West, those of North Africa and Spain, which both enjoyed long and rich ecclesiastical traditions, were probably the two most autonomous from Rome. Thus, the dramatic social changes that open the 700s would both turn the Christian world northward and reinforce greater dependence on Rome in the West.

By the middle of the century, two events occurred that left their mark on the ministry of the bishop of Rome. The first was the decision of Pope Zachary (741–752) to ally himself with the Franks in the West rather than continue to depend on the emperor of Constantinople for protection against the constant threats of the Lombards.[22] Zachary supported the

---

[22] Horst Fuhrmann, "Theoretical and Practical Renewals of the Primacy of Rome: 2, From the Early Middle Ages until the Gregorian Reform," *Concilium* 64 (1971): 54–61, at 55. Fuhrmann adds that, at the time, Zachary was in "imminent danger of being executed by the Byzan-

coronation of Pepin in 751, who in turn was encouraged by Pope Stephen II (752–757) to recover for the bishops of Rome the land within central Italy currently occupied by the Lombards. This action could be justified as a recovery of what rightfully belonged to the bishops of Rome because of the legendary "Donation of Constantine," which stems from this period and claims that the first Christian emperor had given various western territories to Pope Sylvester (314–335) in thanksgiving for having baptized him and cured him of leprosy. The defeat of the Lombards in 774 paved the way for the beginnings of the papal states, which continued in existence for over a thousand years. Charlemagne's coronation by the pope in St. Peter's basilica on Christmas Day of 800 would further reinforce the shift by which the political and social direction of the West had less and less to do with Constantinople and the East. This shift would influence the development of relations between the pope and the bishops insofar as that relation would develop during the second millennium in nearly total isolation from the great churches of the East.

To these political changes should be added the continuation of missionary activity in the North, particularly by the Anglo-Saxon Wynfrith, later known as Boniface (ca. 675–754). Boniface left England for Rome in 718 hoping to be entrusted with a mission from the pope. Gregory II (715–731) obliged, sending him to the region comprised of various Germanic territories (Frisia, Hesse, Thuringia, Bavaria). His thirty-five-year missionary career would involve him in efforts to reform the Frankish church as well. Boniface saw himself as an "ambassador of St. Peter" and made a special oath of loyalty to the pope, not unlike that required of newly consecrated bishops in the areas nearer to Rome. He continually asked advice and direction from the popes, believing that order and reform of the church could only be

---

tine emperor," with whom he had clashed over the problem of iconoclasm.

achieved in closest cooperation with the center of unity and its tradition. His Rome-centeredness coincided with the beginnings of a devotion to Peter among many northern Christians. Rome grew as a major center for pilgrimages, something that it had long been for Eastern Christians in earlier centuries. This attraction of Rome now blossomed in the North, even to the extent that "four Anglo-Saxon kings in the seventh and eighth centuries humbly resigned their thrones and went on pilgrimage to Rome to end their lives there."[23]

The major doctrinal controversy of the eighth century has roots that are not easy to discern. Possibly because of the influence of his new Muslim neighbors or possibly out of deference to the temperamental preferences of his soldiers, the Byzantine emperor Leo III in ca. 724 began to support a movement, shared by a number of bishops from Asia Minor, against the veneration of images. Later emperors followed his footsteps, and the movement soon came to be known as "iconoclasm." It was immediately resisted by the patriarch of Constantinople, Germanus, who was soon forced to resign, and by a succession of popes, one of whom called a synod in Rome which condemned iconoclasm in 731. The emperor retaliated in 733 by removing Illyricum, southern Italy, and Sicily from the ecclesiastical jurisdiction of the popes and assigning them to the new patriarch of Constantinople, who was his supporter. The Council of Hiereia was held in 754 for the purpose of providing a doctrinal basis for iconoclasm. Christological reasons were adduced to argue that the veneration of images was idolatrous. Only with the accession of the emperor Constantine VI, guided by his mother, Empress Irene, was a council able to be held (II Nicaea) in 787, which rejected iconoclasm and ruled in favor of the veneration of images. The relevance of II Nicaea for the question of primacy appears in its consideration of the reasons for rejecting the synod of Hiereia, which had pur-

---

[23] Schatz, *Papal Primacy,* 65.

ported to be an ecumenical council. The Roman delegate John stated that Hiereia was invalid:

> because neither the Roman pope nor the bishops around him cooperated in it, either through delegates or letters, which is the law of councils. But even the patriarchs of the East, from Alexandria, Antioch and the Holy City did not approve it.[24]

Cooperation by the bishop of Rome is presented here as one of the elements of "the law of councils," which seems also to require the approval of the patriarchs of the East. Later Patriarch Nicephorus of Constantinople, in writing about the validity of II Nicaea, would refer to the need for Rome's participation for a doctrinal definition: "Without them [Roman delegates] no dogma can receive definitive approbation . . . for they preside over the episcopal office and they have received this dignity from the two leading apostles."[25]

Toward the Second Millennium

During the ninth century two factors seem particularly important for the exercise of primacy, especially in relation to episcopacy. In the West, Charlemagne (742–814) predicated his empire on a close harmony between church and state, which was to begin to break down into tensions not long after his death. Building on reforms that had been begun by St. Boniface in the previous century, Charlemagne renewed the metropolitan system of episcopal organization, which had fallen into disuse under the royal control of the church by the Frankish kings. However, the reestablished metropolitan system did not succeed in recapturing collegial spirit among bishops which had marked the synodical func-

---

[24] Mansi, 13:208–9. That there must be a cooperation and harmony between a council and the primate for a synod to be considered truly ecumenical, see V. Peri, "La synergie entre le pape et le concile oecuménique: Note d'histoire sur l'ecclésiologie traditionelle de l'Église indivise," in *Irénikon* 56 (1983): 163–93.

[25] Migne, *PG*, 100:597A–B.

tioning of ecclesial structure in the earlier centuries. The net
result was to place the suffragan bishops, that is, those under
a metropolitan archbishop, in an even more subservient
position, subject to the sometimes quite arbitrary authority
not only of secular rulers but also of the metropolitan archbishops. Within this situation there appeared what since the
seventeenth century have been called the Pseudo-Isidorian
Decretals, able to be dated rather precisely to between the
years 847 and 857 by means of internal and external evidence.[26] These forgeries presented themselves as a collection
of decretals that had been promulgated by popes and councils from the time of Clement I (d. 90) to that of Gregory II
(d. 731). They touched upon many aspects of ecclesial life,
but most of all upon legal norms governing accusations and
ecclesial trials, especially as directed against bishops. The
Pseudo-Isidorian Decretals (attributed to Isidore Mercator,
though often during the later Middle Ages simply presumed
to have been principally compiled by St. Isidore of Seville
[560–636]) made it difficult if not impossible for a secular
ruler or a metropolitan to depose a bishop without approval
of the pope. In fact, the occasion to which many attribute the
origin of the False Decretals is the struggle between suffragan bishops and Hincmar of Rheims in the mid-ninth
century. To the bishop of Rome belonged the final word concerning judgments about bishops as well as the ratification
of councils and synods. This concentration of authority in
the pope would be further enhanced by the use of the *pallium*, a symbol of the metropolitan's supra-diocesan authority which was granted directly by the bishop of Rome and by
the progressive practice, already begun in the missionary
activity in England and Germany during the previous two

---

[26] See Y. Congar, "Les fausses décrétales, leur réception, leur influence," in *Église et papauté* (Paris: Cerf, 1994), 81–92; and G. Hartmann,
Der Primat des römischen Bischofs bei Pseudo-Isidor (Stuttgart:
Kohlhammer, 1930); and A. Marchetto, *Episcopato e Primato pontificio
nelle decretali Pseudo Isidoriane* (Rome: Pont. Univ. Lateranense, 1971).

centuries, by which it fell to the pope to set up new dioceses and ecclesiastical boundaries.

Finally, the "eighth" ecumenical council took place in Constantinople in 869–870, precisely one thousand years prior to Vatican I, the first council recognized as ecumenical by the West but not by the East.[27] At its heart was the dispute between two rival candidates for the role of patriarch of Constantinople: Ignatius and Photius.[28] Both appealed for support to the bishop of Rome, Nicholas I, who eventually sided with Ignatius. Emperor Michael III, however, supported Photius and even sought to depose Nicholas in 867. After the new emperor who had succeeded to the throne, the council (IV Constantinople) was held to depose Photius and to reinstate Ignatius. Canon 21 of the council reaffirms the primatial status of the five sees, showing special deference to the bishop of Rome, seemingly in response to the action of Emperor Michael.

> no secular powers should treat with disrespect any of those who hold the office of patriarch or seek to move them from their high positions, but rather they should esteem them as worthy of all honour and reverence. This applies in the first place to the most holy pope of old Rome, secondly to the patriarch of Constantinople, and then to the patriarchs of Alexandria, Antioch and Jerusalem. Furthermore, nobody else should compose or edit writings or tracts against the most holy pope of old Rome, on the pretext to making incriminating charges, as Photius did recently and Dioscorus a long time ago. Whoever shows such great arrogance and audacity, after the manner of Photius and Dioscorus, and makes false accusations in writing or speech against the see of Peter, the chief of the apostles, let him receive a punishment equal to theirs.[29]

---

[27] See V. Peri, "C'è un concilio oecumenico ottavo?" *Annuarium Historiae Conciliorum* 8 (1976): 53–79.

[28] One of the most cited works on this controversy is F. Dvornik, *The Photian Schism: History and Legend* (Cambridge: Cambridge University Press, 1948).

[29] Tanner, *Decrees of the Ecumenical Councils*, 1:182.

While this canon speaks of the arrogance of making false accusations against the pope, some might see a degree of papal arrogance in another event associated with this council. The papal legates required those bishops who had supported Photius to sign a *libellus satisfactionis* if they wished to retain their sees, a text very similar to the Formula of Hormisdas in 519, which acknowledged in no uncertain terms the primacy of the bishop of Rome. The head of the Roman delegation, Anastasius, secretly had copies made of these signed documents. When the ship carrying the official delegation back to Rome was attacked by pirates, who seemed strangely interested in robbing the conciliar documents, the copies were safely transferred to Rome in another vessel.

Canon 21 concluded with the following statement about how questions concerning the church or bishop of Rome should be taken up by an ecumenical council:

> if a universal synod is held and any question or controversy arises about the holy church of Rome, it should make inquiries with proper reverence and respect about the question raised and should find a profitable solution; it must on no account pronounce sentence rashly against the supreme pontiffs of old Rome.[30]

It might be observed that, during the first millennium, the sees whose doctrines and bishops were the focus of discussion at the ecumenical councils, by and large, were the great sees of the East: Alexandria, Antioch, and Constantinople. While one should not underestimate the condemnation of Pope Honorius by the sixth council, still it seems undeniable that he misguidedly supported a scheme for reestablishing unity with the Chalcedonians that he himself did not originate and the doctrinal implications of which he did not sufficiently grasp. One could not fairly associate his name with monothelitism in the same way that Arius, Nestorius, and Eutyches are associated with the heresies that bear their

---

[30] Ibid.

names. Some critics have even taunted that Rome was too intellectually backward to give birth to a serious heresy. At any rate, here, during the final ecumenical council of the millennium, one finds a strong affirmation of the special position of the church of Rome in relation to councils and a prohibition of any "rash" sentence against Rome's bishop. At this point in history, such a prohibition might seem rather superfluous, for, in the final analysis, there was no clash between the ecumenical councils and the bishops of Rome during the first millennium. If anything, "the supreme pontiffs of old Rome" ended up playing an indispensable role in ensuring that the councils faithfully preserved the apostolic faith, delivered once for all to the church and spoken by the lips of Peter, prompting Jesus' church-founding logion of Matthew 16. It would be well into the second millennium before an apparent opposition between pope and council in the guise of conciliarism would first see the light of day.

IV Constantinople ended in 870. It was followed by the term of a rather strong bishop of Rome, John VIII (872–882). But after John came the deluge. The *saeculum obscurum,* or dark century, of the papacy turned out to last quite a bit longer than a century—not only the entire tenth but well into the eleventh. It was also a period of continued estrangement between Rome and the churches of the East. By the time that Pope Leo IX (1049–1054) began to set the house back in order, relations with the East had so deteriorated that the mutual excommunications by Cardinal Humbert of Silva Candida and Patriarch of Constantinople Michael Cerularius in 1054 were able to stick, causing an unfortunate division that is still not overcome even today, despite the marvelous gesture of Pope Paul VI and Patriarch Athenagoras, when, in 1965, they committed those ancient mutual anathemas to oblivion.

CHAPTER 5

Libertas ecclesiae:
The Reform of Gregory VII

Few would doubt that the reforms promoted by the popes of the middle of the eleventh century, culminating in the pontificate of Gregory VII (1073–1085), were directed at bettering a situation that was in dire need of improvement. These reforms followed 150 years in which nearly fifty different persons had served as bishop of Rome. Often they had assumed that ministry under circumstances which were less than edifying, and their pastoral guidance of the church was scarcely discernible.[1] This lack of leadership created a situation throughout Western Christianity that called for serious reform. However, reform was effectively frustrated by the fact that the selection of bishops was largely in the hands of secular rulers, a consequence of the feudal system that had been in place for some centuries. In this situation, the conception of the primacy was about to undergo a decisive modification, which is summarized by Klaus Schatz in this way:

> It became no longer simply the center of Church unity, the norm of true belief, and the measure of authentic tradition. Now, for the first time, the papacy became truly the head of the Church, from it went forth all important decisions, and within it all the functions of the life of the whole Church were coordinated. Now Rome raised (and enforced), to a far

---

[1] See Y. Congar, "De la communion des églises a une ecclésiologie de l'Église universelle," in *L'Épiscopat et l'Église universelle*, ed. Y. Congar and B. D. Dupuy, Unam Sanctam 39 (Paris: Cerf, 1962), 227–60, at 237. Congar also notes the virtual lack of any reference to doctrinal contributions by these popes in a collection such as that of Denzinger.

greater degree than before, the claim to play an active role in shaping the life of the Church and determining the way it should go—thus not merely by responding to questions or petitions, which until that time had constituted by far the greater part of papal activity outside the ecclesiastical province of Rome.[2]

This more active direction by the bishop of Rome could only be carried out on the basis of a strong affirmation of papal authority. Already Peter Damian (1007–1072) had called the pope the "universal bishop," a title that, as we have earlier noted, Gregory the Great rejected precisely because it tended to diminish the dignity of other bishops. Peter Damian also described the Roman church as the foundation (*fundamentum*) and pedestal (*basis*) of the church as a whole. His contemporary, Cardinal Humbert of Silva Candida, used the terms head (*caput*), mother (*mater*), hinge (*cardo*) and source (*fons*) to characterize the relation between the church of Rome and the other local churches.[3] This terminology suggests that everything that is decisive about the church, the very quality of being church, comes to the local churches through the mediation of the church of Rome, because of the latter's foundation in Peter, upon whom the church as a whole was founded (Matt. 16:18–19). The application of these words to the church of Rome was not an innovation of the writers of the eleventh century; these ideas had all appeared at one time or another in earlier papal writings. What is new now is their coalescence into a single configuration, suggesting not only that Rome is the unifying point of reference for the other churches, but even their source and origin. The primacy becomes the hinge in the understanding of the church, the source of its life.

Such claims for the church of Rome were not simply arro-

---

[2] K. Schatz, *Papal Primacy: From Its Origins to the Present* (Collegeville, Minn.: Liturgical Press, 1996), 78.

[3] For the use of this terminology by these authors, see Yves Congar, *HDG* III 3c, 56–58, especially n. 28.

gant self-appropriations of power, but rather were thought to
rest ultimately upon a christological basis. St. Paul had taught
that the church is the one body of Christ: Christ is its head,
and from him its life flows. In Peter, upon whom Christ
founded the church, and in Peter's successors, Christ contin-
ues to exercise his headship. The title "Vicar of Christ" eventually became restricted to the pope as his proper title.[4] As
Vicar of Christ, he naturally enjoyed the fullness of power,
the *plenitudo potestatis*. This expression derived from Leo
the Great's letter to Anastasius, his vicar in Thessalonica.
Originally it seemed to apply only to that quite unique relationship in which Anastasius took Leo's place, receiving a
share of the latter's concern for all the churches (*pars sollicitudinis*; cf. 2 Cor. 11:28). Now the expression seems to intend
that every local bishop is a "vicar" to the pope, concerned
with that part of the church which has been apportioned to
him (*in partem sollicitudinis*).[5]

This vision of papal ministry was put decisively into practice by Gregory VII, whose famous reform brought in such
centralizing measures as the codification of laws concerning
dispensations, the unification of liturgical rites, the requirement that archbishops receive the *pallium* in Rome from the
pope and make a profession of faith within three months of
their elections, the increased practice of exemption for
monasteries, which thus would owe their allegiance directly

---

[4] On the gradual restriction of the title "Vicar of Christ" to the pope,
see M. Maccarrone, *Vicarius Christi: Storia del titolo papale* (Rome: Fac.
Theol. Pont. Athenaei Lateranensis, 1952). By the time of Innocent III, the
title "Vicar of Christ" is used not so much in the sacramental sense, which
was predominant in the first millennium, of rendering actually present the
action of an invisible, higher authority—that of Christ or of Peter—but
now in a juridical sense of having received, through succession, the powers of Christ who is corporally absent. See Congar, "La collegialità dell'
episcopato e il primato del vescovo di Roma nella storia," in *Ministeri e
comunione ecclesiale* (Bologna: Edizioni Dehoniane, 1973), 96-97.

[5] See J. Rivière, "*In partem sollicitudinis*: Évolution d'une formule
pontificale," *Revue des sciences religieuses* 5 (1925): 210–31.

to Rome and not to the local bishops, and the widening of the institution and use of papal legates, whose authority was placed above that of bishops and metropolitans.[6] To these measures can be added Gregory's famous *Dictatus Papae* (1075), a series of twenty-seven claims of papal authority, some of which emphasize as papal prerogatives the power to form dioceses and to remove, reinstate, and transfer local bishops.[7] Many canonists and theologians of the twelfth and thirteenth centuries likewise emphasized the pope's unique authority within the church.[8] How does this affect the relationship between primacy and episcopacy?

Freedom from Civil Rulers in Choosing Bishops

One of the defining concerns of the Gregorian reform was the pope's struggle against the lay investiture of bishops. Gregory encouraged canonists to gather together laws from the past that would demonstrate the pope's authority to

---

[6] See Congar, *HDG* III 3c, 64 with references.

[7] The following claims of the *Dictatus* directly affect the relation between the pope and the bishops: (III) that the pope alone can depose or reinstate bishops; (IV) that his legate, even if of a lower rung in the hierarchy, ranks above and can pronounce a decision against all the other bishops; (VII) that it belongs to him alone to make new laws when needed, to set up boundaries, to unite or divide the temporal goods of the episcopacy; (XIII) that he can transfer bishops if necessary; (XVI) that no general council can be called without his command; (XVII) that no chapter can be held without his authority; (XXI) that the principal court cases (*causae maiores*) of all the churches should be referred to him; (XXV) that he can depose or reinstate bishops without convoking a council. The critical text of the *Dictatus Papae* can be found in E. Caspar, *Das Register Gregors VII*, *MGH*, *Epistolae Selectae* II,1 (Berlin: Weidmann, 1920), 202–8. Various hypotheses have been proposed as their origin; the most creditable seems to be that they were intended as chapter headings for a collection of older canons which Gregory VII directed his canonists to compile.

[8] See Congar, *HDG* III 3c, 77–80 on Bernard of Clairvaux; pp. 92–95 on Gratian; pp. 99–102 on Hugh of St. Victor and Peter Lombard; p. 125 on Innocent III; p. 144 on Bonaventure; and pp. 154–55 on Thomas Aquinas.

defend the freedom of the church to select bishops without interference from secular rulers. It was not primarily the freedom of the *pope* that was at issue, but rather the freedom of those traditionally responsible for electing bishops, the cathedral chapters of the local churches. It is instructive that the *Dictatus Papae* do not speak of the pope's power to appoint bishops, but only to depose or reinstate or transfer them. Since the local churches were dominated by secular authorities and lacked the power to fulfill their traditional role, the pope championed their rightful freedom. Gregory did not intend to transfer to himself the authority that had wrongly been usurped by secular lords.

The pope was able to do this by emphasizing his own authority on the basis of the ancient canons.[9] The action of collecting laws from the past indicates that Gregory VII's emphasis was not upon "creating" new canons, even though one of the sentences of the *Dictatus Papae* does affirm his authority to establish new laws according to the needs of the time.[10] Rather, his basic aim was to reform current practice on the basis of what had already been established in the past. Only in the thirteenth century was emphasis placed on the distinction between "divine law," which no human authority could change, and "ecclesiastical law," over which the pope was seen as having almost unlimited authority. Instead Gregory wanted to identify and be faithful to what was the true tradition of the church, eliminating aberrations that had crept in, such as lay investiture.[11] These developments give

---

[9] Our last chapter acknowledged that some collections of "ancient canons," especially the Pseudo-Isidorian Decretals, which strongly empowered the pope to supervise cases involving the removal of suffragan bishops, turned out to be forgeries. The incontrovertible demonstration of this fact in the early 1600s would occasion later thinkers, such as the proponents of Gallicanism, to argue that papal primacy really entailed a much more limited authority than what had been claimed for it since the time of Gregory VII.

[10] See n. 7 above.

[11] So Schatz, *Papal Primacy*, 87–88.

rise to two questions about papal primacy: first, its relation to canon law, and, second, its role in the election of bishops.

Primacy and Law

Catholic ecclesiologists from the twentieth century such as Yves Congar and Angel Antón frequently have lamented the fact that, with the Gregorian reform, a fundamentally juridical vision begins to predominate the way in which the church is understood in the West.[12] Congar goes so far as to suggest that only with Vatican II have the Catholic ecclesiology and doctrine begun to free themselves from the dominance of this juridical view and to adopt the more original and more theologically adequate sacramental understanding of the church. A possible rejoinder to Congar might be that, in the situation of the eleventh century, recourse to law was the only possible way in which the pope could act effectively to defend the freedom of the local churches in selecting bishops. By promoting such freedom, the Gregorian reform was supporting the intimate relation between the local church and its bishop and consequently was strengthening one of the most important pillars within the sacramental vision of the church. Gregory's emphasis on canon law sought not to replace the more original sacramental vision of the church but, in a way, to defend it in the face of manipulation by civil rulers who had little interest in providing effective ministry for God's people. That being said, one may nevertheless wonder whether the juridical means used to achieve this end may not ultimately have overshadowed the desired effect. The desired freedom was won, but the fundamental "sacramentality" of the church was somewhat forgotten in the face

---

[12] Congar, *HDG* III 3c, 65–68; idem, "La collegialità dell'episcopato," 94–100; idem, "The Historical Development of Authority in the Church," in *Problems of Authority*, ed. John M. Todd (Baltimore/London: Helicon, 1962), 119–55; A. Antón, *El misterio de la Iglesia* (Madrid/Toledo: BAC, 1986, 1987), 1:171–74.

of the overriding insistence that the church is a juridically structured society. In the midst of the pressing needs of the eleventh century, law served the primacy, helping it to reaffirm the right relation between the local church and its bishop. But did it do more than that? Did recourse to law in some way alter both the primacy as well as the predominant way in which the church understood itself in the West?

Selecting Bishops

The Gregorian reform suggests that the primacy has a duty and a right to promote the freedom of local churches in selecting bishops. Thus, the practice of the *pope*'s selecting bishops for local churches would not flow from the Gregorian reform but rather would seem to run counter to it. Yet papal appointment of bishops was practiced increasingly for various reasons, some positive and others negative. Positively, popes intervened as a necessary court of appeal in the local selection of bishops when that process failed to function, especially when local electors did not succeed in agreeing on a candidate.[13] Negatively, especially at the time of the Avignon papacy, financial considerations sometimes led to an increase in the practice of papal appointment of bishops.[14] In subsequent centuries, other factors favored such papal initiative—for example, the direction by the see of Rome of the missionary activity of the Catholic Church outside of Europe after the beginning of the sixteenth century

---

[13] Part II, section 9 of the Second Council of Lyon (1274) is but one witness to this recourse to the bishop of Rome in the case of disputed elections; see Tanner, *Decrees of the Ecumenical Councils*, 1:320–21. Part II, sections 5–12 of II Lyon are all concerned principally with the local election of bishops, thus showing that this was the common practice two hundred years after the time of Gregory VII.

[14] B. Tierney states that, during the Avignon period, the selection of bishops by the pope was a source of considerable income for the papal curia ("Pope and Bishops before Trent: An Historical Survey," in *The Papacy and the Church in the United States* [Mahwah, N.J.: Paulist Press, 1989], 20–21).

and especially after the foundation of the office of the *Propaganda fidei* to direct Catholic missions in the early seventeenth century.[15] These developments notwithstanding, it seems that the selection of local bishops was never proposed as an essential element of the primatial ministry as such. The predominant practice of the church, not only in the first millennium but even in much of the second, suggests otherwise.

Power of Order and Power of Jurisdiction

The distinction between the powers of order and jurisdiction is of fundamental importance for the way in which primacy and episcopacy came to be related in the West.[16] The distinction as such seems never to have been introduced either in practice or in theory in the East.[17] Behind the emergence of this distinction lie specific problems, such as the question of the validity of sacraments celebrated by an ordained minister whose tie of communion with the church was broken (an issue going back as far as St. Cyprian) and the question of the so-called absolute ordinations (ordination without reference to ministry in a specific community), which were forbidden by the Council of Chalcedon, but which eventually imposed themselves upon the life of the church, at least in the West.[18] By the time of the Gregorian reform and in sub-

---

[15] J. Hennesey gives a good example of this when he shows that the designation of the church in the United States as a mission assured that its bishops would be appointed by Rome ("Rome and the Origins of the United States Hierarchy," in *The Papacy and the Church in the United States* [Mahwah, N.J.: Paulist Press, 1989], 79–97).

[16] So J. Ratzinger, "La collegialità episcopale dal punto di vista teologico," in *La Chiesa del Vaticano II*, ed. G. Baraúna (Florence: Vallecchi, 1965), 737; and Antón, *El misterio de la Iglesia*, 1:171.

[17] So P. Anciaux, "L'Épiscopat (ordo episcoporum) come réalité sacramentelle," *Nouvelle Revue de Théologie* 85 (1963): 156; Antón, *El misterio de la Iglesia*, 1:172; and G. Dejaifve, "Le premier des évêques," *Nouvelle Revue de Théologie* 82 (1960): 575–76.

[18] See Antón, *El misterio de la Iglesia*, 1:172; and Y. Congar, "Ordre et juridiction dans l'Église," in his *Sainte Église* (Paris: Cerf, 1963), 203–37.

sequent centuries, this question came into sharp relief
because of the need to clarify the ministerial status of monks
or other vowed religious who were ordained but whose
ministry was not assigned to any specific parochial community. In order to describe the situation of such ordained
ministers, Gratian's influential decretals (ca. 1140) distinguished between the power of orders and its exercise. By
ordination these priests enjoyed the power to exercise sacramental ministry but they had no authority to do so within a
particular community. Within about fifty years, Gratian's
ordo-executio distinction developed into the distinction
between order and jurisdiction.[19] The distinction gained
widespread acceptance, and its legitimacy has been commonly presupposed by canonists and theologians in the West
ever since. Already in the thirteenth century, such an eminent
theologian as Thomas Aquinas wrote:

> Spiritual power is twofold: the one sacramental, the other a
> power of jurisdiction. The sacramental power is one that is
> conferred by some kind of consecration. Now all the conse-
> crations of the Church are immovable so long as the conse-
> crated thing remains. . . . Consequently such a power as this
> remains, as to its essence, in the man who has received it by
> consecration, as long as he lives, even if he fall into schism or
> heresy. . . . On the other hand, the power of jurisdiction is
> that which is conferred by a mere human appointment of a
> man. Such a power as this does not adhere to the recipient
> immovably. . . .[20]

Canon 6 from Chalcedon forbidding the ordination of "any cleric without title" is found in Tanner, *Decrees of the Ecumenical Councils*, 1:90.

[19] See E. Corecco, "L'origine del potere di giurisdizione episcopale:
Aspetti storico-giuridici e metodologico-sistematici della questione," *La
Scuola cattolica* 96 (1968): 6–18, 35–52, 118–19; and J. J. Ryan, *The Sep-
aration of 'Ordo' and 'Iurisdictio' in its Structural-Doctrinal Development and Ecclesiological Significance* (diss., Münster, 1972). A. Carrasco
Rouco provides a fine presentation of contemporary Catholic reflection
on the origin of the distinction between order and jurisdiction (*Le primat
de l'évêque de Rome* [Fribourg: Editions Universitaires, 1990], 117–30).

[20] *Summa theologica*, II-II 39, 3. Translation taken from the Fathers of

Jurisdiction entails the granting of authority to exercise ordained ministry in a particular portion of the flock of Christ. The distinction between order and jurisdiction supposes, as the citation from Aquinas indicates, that ordination (*consecratio*) as such does not convey an assignment to a specific community. This is precisely where the distinction enters into the relation between primacy and episcopacy. Since the primatial ministry is specifically directed to the maintenance of the good order of the whole church, the pope is seen as the one who provides jurisdiction to the bishops by assigning to each of them that portion of the flock to which he must minister.[21] The profound link between the papacy and the granting of jurisdiction is captured in the often quoted sentence of Augustinus Triumphus from the early 1300s: *Papa est nomen iurisdictionis.*[22]

In this conception, bishops are obviously quite dependent on the pope; their authority is mediated through him. Innocent III shows how far this idea can be pushed. While admitting that the power of the keys was given both to Peter (Matthew 16) and to the apostles (Matthew 18), he observed that Peter was with the apostles in the second instance, while that power was entrusted to Peter alone in the first. From this Innocent III concluded that the text about Christ in John 1:16—"from his fullness we have all received"—could also be applied to the papacy.[23] While the position of Thomas Aquinas seems to be more nuanced, nevertheless he too would write:

---

the English Dominican Province, *St. Thomas Aquinas: Summa Theologica*, vol. 2 (New York: Benziger Brothers, 1947), 1358.

[21] Justifications of this idea went so far as to propose that St. Peter himself had assigned territories to the individual apostles; see Y. Congar, "Notes sur le destin de l'idée de collégialité épiscopale en Occident au Moyen Age (VIIᵉ-XVIᵉ siècles)," in *La collégialité épiscopale* (Paris: Cerf, 1965), 114–15.

[22] Congar, *HDG* III 3c, 94. The word *nomen* here means the fundamental characteristic of a person or an office. Thus, the sense of this saying is: "To be pope means to have or to exercise jurisdiction."

[23] Ibid., III 3c, 125–26.

Although the power of binding and loosing was given to all of the apostles together, nevertheless, so that the order in this power might be denoted, it was first given to Peter alone, so that it would be clear that this power must descend from him to the others, which is why to him alone he [Christ] said: Confirm your brothers (Luke 22:32) and Feed my sheep (John 21:17). (*IV Sent.* d. 24, q. 3, a. 2, sol. 3)

This leads a more one-sided defender of papal primacy such as Juan of Torquemada (1400s) to assert that the Roman pontiff is the "fountain-like source of all ecclesiastical power" (*fontalis origo totius potestatis ecclesiasticae*).[24]

Georges Dejaifve has pointed out that, while the view that the pope supplies jurisdiction to all the bishops has reigned supreme in Catholic thought for centuries, it is not illegitimate to ask whether this belongs to the very essence of the primacy, or whether it may be simply the way in which the primacy came to be understood and exercised within the concrete circumstances that conditioned the church in the West.[25] Perhaps this should constitute an important issue for dialogue about the primacy in the future. Here some positive and negative consequences of the order/jurisdiction theme can be pointed out. From the positive side, it is clear that the unity of the church requires some coordination of the exercise of ministry. That the ministry of primacy should serve the unity of the church by having some voice, even determinative if the case warrant, in this coordination of ministry would seem to be a logical and even necessary dimension of the primacy. From the negative side, however, the view that only the bishop of Rome can grant to all the other bishops the jurisdiction to shepherd their particular churches suggests that the church may be understood as if it were one huge diocese. The care of a particular part is assigned by the

---

[24] See Antón, *El misterio de la Iglesia*, 1:179. In Torquemada's *Summa de Ecclesia* 1.2 c. 55, he writes of the two powers, following very closely the comment from St. Thomas given above (*Summa Theologica* II-II 39, 3).

[25] Dejaifve, "Le premier des évêques," 575.

one who is pastor of the whole. The individual bishop is considered practically to be a vicar to the pope. Would such a view sufficiently guard against forgetting that Christ is the one shepherd and that the bishops are vicars of Christ? Moreover, this view tends to isolate the individual bishop, limiting him to his specific portion of the church. That the bishops together and even individually have some responsibility for the unity of the church as a whole is at best obscured, at worst lost. It is perhaps important not to lose sight of the fact that the theological and canonical opinion that all jurisdiction flowed from the pope was never finally adopted by the ecumenical councils held in the West during the second millennium.

Cardinals, Friars, and Councils

Several other developments during this period should be briefly mentioned since they affect the relation between primacy and episcopacy. First, there is the gradual refinement of the college of cardinals as the body charged with electing the pope.[26] Two positive aspects of this development are (1) the generally successful way in which this college has carried out the election of the bishop of Rome and (2) the fact that, since the cardinals were seen as representatives of the local church of Rome, the pope was understood precisely as the bishop of a local church. As such, the pope is, first of all, brother to all the other bishops of local churches. His primacy is related to the "more powerful origin" (*potentior principatus*), to use the expression of St. Irenaeus, of the local church of Rome. From the negative side, however, the collegial nature of the college of cardinals tended to obscure the fact that the whole episcopate forms a college. Various theories arose that proposed that the "college" represented by Peter and the apostles in the New Testament found con-

---

[26] For an extensive survey of these details, see G. Alberigo, *Cardinalato e collegialità* (Florence: Vallecchi, 1969).

temporary expression in the pope united with the college of cardinals, while individual bishops were the contemporary expression of the apostles dispersed in mission throughout the world.[27] This development contributed to a loss of the sense of episcopal collegiality among the bishops themselves and within ecclesiology.[28]

Second, the emergence of the mendicant orders, which were in their own right structured more along the lines of the universal church and less along the lines of the local churches, had an impact on the relation between primacy and episcopacy. From the positive side, it would seem legitimate that many individuals could be inspired by a common evangelical ideal and that such groups could organize themselves in a worldwide community that extends beyond a single diocese or group of dioceses. Moreover, this type of religious community corresponded to the sociological changes that were occurring in the twelfth and thirteenth centuries, which allowed for greater mobility and for the development of a sense of community that was not restricted to the environs of one city. Naturally, it fell to the pope to approve, regulate, and be the primary ecclesial authority for these supradiocesan communities. Such communities could serve the papacy in its efforts to promote widespread reform within the church. As one might expect, the theologians of these communities, who turned out to be the greatest theologians of high scholasticism, tended to defend papal prerogatives even at the expense of the rights of the local bishops. Negatively, these communities (principally Dominicans, Franciscans, Augustinians, and Carmelites, though later many other orders would adopt a strongly centralized structure, most

---

[27] See Congar, "Notes sur le destin de l'idée de collégialité épiscopale," in *La collégialité épiscopale* (Paris: Cerf, 1965), 99–129.

[28] On the other hand, B. Tierney (*Foundations of the Conciliar Theory* [Cambridge: Cambridge University Press, 1955]) and others see the cardinalate as keeping something of the "collegial" idea alive within the Catholic Church, even preparing the way for conciliarism, which would later appear in the fourteenth and fifteenth centuries.

notably the Jesuits) seemed to interfere with or even disrupt the local direction of church life, which was the prerogative of the bishops.[29] The struggles between the bishops and the pope over the ministerial exemptions given to these communities, a good example of which was the attempt to limit their number and privileges at such councils as II Lyon (1274) or Vienne (1311–1312), ultimately led to a working arrangement in which "exempt" communities were not allowed to exercise ministry in local churches without some subordination to local bishops. Perhaps the final outcome in this question of exemption can be seen as an attempt to bring into proper balance the coordination of ministry in a way that respects the proper competencies of the primacy and the local bishops.

A third development concerns the relation between the pope and general councils. This issue arises more precisely somewhat later during the conciliarist response to the crisis which issues from the Western Schism. But the development of the strongly papal general councils from the twelfth to the fourteenth centuries—councils that were very much under the direction of the pope—refashioned the notion of a general council in a way that made them somewhat different from the ecumenical councils of the first millennium. General councils came to be understood more as events in which all of Christendom was represented so as to provide counsel and support for the pope in his role of directing the activity of the whole. Again, this emphasis on the papacy tended to diminish the authority of the bishops as teachers of the faith and as shepherds of the flock of Christ.

---

[29] Johann J. Ignaz von Döllinger (1799–1890), the German Catholic historian who sharply criticized Vatican I and helped to organize the "Old Catholic" church comprised of Catholics who did not accept that council, wrote in 1869 that, after the decretals of Pseudo-Isidore and Gratian, the foundation of the mendicant orders was the principal means by which what was left of the ancient church was destroyed and buried; cited in Y. Congar, "De la communion des Églises a une ecclésiologie de l'Église universelle," in *L'Épiscopat et l'Église universelle,* 240.

In the end, it is not easy to arrive at an unambiguous evaluation of the events and ecclesiological doctrines that began with the Gregorian reform and unfolded over the next two centuries. Historians of ecclesiology tend to point out that, notwithstanding any of its positive gains, this reform bore the negative marks of diminishing the authority of the local bishop in favor of increasing the authority of the pope. It caused a shift in the "center of gravity" of ecclesiology, away from considering the church predominantly in terms of its sacramentality and its embodiment in the local church to an emphasis on the universality of the church as a juridically structured whole. It is perhaps in no way of secondary importance that this entire period begins with the felt need for a reform of the *whole* church. Where the whole becomes the focus of attention, either in disciplinary or doctrinal matters, it is almost inevitable that primacy will have to play a significant or even dominant role. Moreover, in the pair primacy-episcopacy, it is difficult to emphasize the authority of the one without in some way apparently or effectively diminishing the authority of the other.

Looking ahead to the next three chapters, it is difficult to avoid the impression that the three high points in the subsequent history—conciliarism, Vatican I, and Vatican II—are rather predictable developments in working out the tensions that already emerge in our analysis of the reform of Gregory VII. With conciliarism, the pendulum swings back in the direction of episcopal authority; Vatican I reaffirms papal primacy to the rejection of certain episcopalist claims; and Vatican II attempts to retrieve episcopal authority and the importance of the local church, now within the context of Vatican I's doctrine of papal primacy and infallibility.

CHAPTER 6

A House Divided:
Schism and Conciliarism

This one and unique Church, therefore, has not two heads,
like a monster, but one body and one head, viz., Christ and
his vicar, Peter's successor, for the Lord said to him personally: "Feed my sheep" (John 21:17). "My" he said in general,
not individually, meaning these or those; whereby it is understood that he confided all his sheep to him. If therefore the
Greeks or others say that they were not confided to Peter and
his successors, they must necessarily confess that they are not
among Christ's sheep, for the Lord said in John: "there shall
be one fold and one shepherd" (John 10:16).[1]

These words from Boniface VIII's bull *Unam sanctam* of
1302 might serve as a summation of the growing tendency
within Catholic ecclesiology that began with the Gregorian
reform. This understanding of the church emphasized its
universal unity as one body with one head. Contemporary to
this papal bull is the appearance of two of the most radical
proponents of the absoluteness of papal power, who proposed what Congar and Antón call a "papal hierocracy," the
Augustinian friars Giles of Rome (1243–1316) and his disciple James of Viterbo (ca. 1255–1308).[2] It is perhaps not

---

[1] DH 872. English translation taken from J. Neuner and J. Dupuis, *The
Christian Faith*, 6th ed. (Bangalore: Theological Publications in India,
1996), 281.

[2] Giles's *De ecclesiastica sive Summi Pontificis potestate* claimed that
the pope enjoyed the height and fullness of all spiritual and temporal

without irony that the period of the Avignon papacy began shortly after the promulgation of *Unam sanctam*, coming to an end only with a schism in which two and then three individuals claimed to be "head" of this one body, almost as if the rather monarchical view of the papacy issuing from the Gregorian reform led to the very "monster" which Boniface's bull decried. Granted that Christ is the one head of his body, can the institutional church be subject to more than one visible head? The question of the ultimate instance of authority within the church on earth is at the very heart of the conciliarist crisis.

The Inadequacy of Conciliarism

Conciliarism is the term used to express the doctrines of a number of theologians of the fourteenth and fifteenth centuries who adopted the position that the authority of a general council is above that of the pope.[3] Moderate conciliarists proposed such superiority of a council over the papacy only when exceptional circumstances warranted it, such as in the case of a schism caused by rival claimants to the papacy or in the case of a pope who deviated into heresy. The more radical conciliarists proposed such superiority of the council even under normal circumstances. Naturally each conciliar-

---

power and went so far as practically to identify the church with the papacy: "the pope, who can be called the church" (*papa, qui potest dici Ecclesia* [II c. 13]). James of Viterbo's *De regimine christiano* made much use of the concept of "kingdom" (*regnum*) to describe the church, emphasizing its pyramid-like structure with the pope at the top. See Congar, *HDG* III 3c, 177–78; and Angel Antón, *El misterio de la Iglesia* (Madrid/Toledo: BAC, 1986, 1987), 1:110–12.

[3] Antón (*El misterio de la Iglesia*, 1:200–260) lists eleven writers who proposed varying forms of conciliarism: Marsilio of Padua (1275/80–1342/43), William of Ockham (1285–1347), John of Paris (d. 1306), Conrad of Gelnhausen (1320–1390), Henry of Langenstein (1340–1397), Peter of Ailly (1350–1420), John Gerson (1363–1429), Francis Zabarella (1360–1417), Nicholas Tudeschi (1386–1445), Nicholas of Cusa (1401–1464), and John of Ragusa (d. 1443).

ist author has his own particular nuances, but common to them all is a recourse to that tradition which, even in the more forceful proponents of papal authority, provided for the possibility that there could be a breakdown in the papacy. This was captured in the fact that, to the traditional maxim *"Papa a nemine iudicandus est"* (the pope is to be judged by no one) was appended the phrase *"nisi deprehendatur a fide devius"* (unless he is caught off the road from the faith).[4] Moreover, the conciliarists were all influenced by the democratic and nationalistic currents that emerged in society in the fourteenth century and which found particularly forceful expression in Marsilio of Padua's political theory and in Ockham's personalism.[5] For the sake of brevity, we will consider here only the substantially similar positions of two of the more prominent of the moderate conciliarists: Peter of Ailly and John Gerson.[6]

Both of these men were of the University of Paris, and both played a significant role in bringing the Western Schism (1378–1415) to an end during the Council of Constance (1414–1418). They understood the church in a strongly christological and pneumatological way. Following the predominant medieval view that the church is first and foremost a *congregatio fidelium*, they understood faith, stirred up and sustained by the Holy Spirit, as the primary source of the church's unity. Christ is the head of the church. But Christ himself instituted the hierarchy to serve ecclesial unity and established the primacy within it as a secondary *caput* of the church. D'Ailly and Gerson both acknowledged that, as such, the pope enjoys the *plenitudo potestatis* within the church and even that this fullness of primatial power is the

---

[4] On this maxim, see G. Dejaifve, "La collegialità nella tradizione latina," in *La Chiesa del Vaticano II*, ed. G. Baraúna (Florence: Vallecchi, 1965), 843.

[5] See Antón, *El misterio de la Iglesia*, 1:112–17.

[6] The following description follows the accounts of Peter of Ailly and John Gerson as presented by Congar, *HDG* III 3d, 14–18; and Antón, *El misterio de la Iglesia*, 1:221–31.

source for the ministerial authority of the rest of the hierarchy. But these divinely established structural dimensions of
the church do not diminish the fact that Christ remains the
primary *caput* of the church and the source of the *plenitudo
potestatis* which is imparted to the church as a whole. In an
ecumenical council, which, as such, represents the church as
a whole, this fullness of power comes into act. In the case of
a schism caused by rival popes, the council has the capacity
to resolve the crisis and thus is above the pope. In this way
(*via concilii*), Christ the supreme head preserves the unity of
his body by acting through the council, which represents the
church as a whole.

For D'Ailly and Gerson, this was precisely what came to
pass in the difficult events that led to and suffused the Council of Constance. The decree *Haec sancta* of April 6, 1415,
was approved by the council at the very tense moment when
the Pisan anti-pope, John XXIII, who had convoked the
council, gave in to second thoughts about losing his power
and took flight, thus jeopardizing the entire effort to end the
schism. The most important sentences of *Haec sancta* read
as follows:

> First it [the holy Synod of Constance] declares that, legiti-
> mately assembled in the holy Spirit, constituting a general
> Council and representing the catholic church militant, it has
> power immediately from Christ; and that everyone of what-
> ever state or dignity, even papal, is bound to obey it in those
> matters which pertain to the faith, the eradication of the said
> schism and the general reform of the said church of God in
> head and members.
>
> Next, it declares that anyone of whatever condition, state
> or dignity, even papal, who contumaciously refuses to obey
> the past or future mandates, statutes, ordinances or precepts
> of this sacred synod or of any other legitimately assembled
> general council, regarding the aforesaid things or matters
> pertaining to them, shall be subjected to well-deserved
> penance, unless he repents, and shall be duly punished. . . .[7]

---

[7] Norman P. Tanner, ed., *Decrees of the Ecumenical Councils* (Washington, D.C.: Georgetown University Press, 1990), 1:409.

These statements clearly affirm a certain superiority of the council, whose authority comes directly from Christ, over the pope, who is bound to obey the decisions of the council concerning faith, the eradication of schism, and the reform of the church. Two questions are often addressed by scholars analyzing *Haec sancta*. First, is *Haec sancta* affirming that radical conciliarism which places conciliar authority always over that of the pope, or is it affirming the moderate conciliarism that sees such superiority as existing only in a situation of crisis? The reference to "any other legitimately congregated council" suggests that *Haec sancta* proposes the more radical view. Nevertheless, the rather extreme circumstances of the dire threat to the success of Constance because of the flight of the one pope who had supported it suggests that the approval of the decree was dominated by the crisis and that it must be understood above all within the context of the need to end the schism, and not as a more serene general statement about the normal relation between a council and the pope.[8] Second, what magisterial authority can be assigned to *Haec sancta*? Is it a conciliar definition which, as such, would seem to be in contradiction with Vatican I's subsequent doctrine of papal primacy? There are several good reasons for questioning such an interpretation, not the least of which is the fact that the council itself later acquiesced in the Roman pope Gregory XII's insistence that he "re-convoke" it as a condition for his cooperation in ending the schism. Such an acquiescence amounts to an admission that, at the time of the approval of *Haec sancta*, Constance was not yet a legitimately congregated council with the authority to promulgate a definition.[9]

What does this have to do with the relation between primacy and episcopacy? On the one hand, it might seem that

---

[8] K. Schatz argues convincingly for this conclusion (*Papal Primacy: From Its Origins to the Present* [Collegeville, Minn.: Liturgical Press, 1996], 111–14).

[9] For other arguments against the legitimacy of *Haec sancta* as a conciliar definition, see Congar, *HDG* III 3d, 20–21.

the conciliarist position raises up the authority of bishops over that of the pope, as least in certain extreme circumstances. But at closer inspection, it appears that neither the conciliarists nor the Council of Constance focused in any substantial way on the ministry of bishops, on their unity as a college, or on the way in which the college of bishops relates to the universal church and to the ministry of the bishop of Rome.[10] Rather their concern was to affirm the authority of the church as a whole, which included therefore also the bishops, in resolving a situation of crisis, even without the cooperation of the pope.

The first stages of the following ecumenical council of Basel-Ferrera-Florence-Rome (1431–1445) tended to affirm the authority of the council over that of the pope and, when Eugene IV transferred the council to Ferrara with a view to facilitating union negotiations with the Eastern churches, a resistance group continued in Basel and espoused the radical form of conciliarism, going so far as to elect a rival pope, Felix V (1439–1449). With this, some of the more reputable proponents of the conciliar ideal, such as Nicholas of Cusa (1401–1464), abandoned the council and went over to the side of Pope Eugene IV. This, along with the fact that the Eastern churches had no interest in reestablishing unity with a part of the West that did not include the bishop of Rome, led to the inevitable defeat of the conciliarists. In the end, however, the deeper reason for their failure seems to be the inherent insufficiency of any view that separates or even opposes the ecumenical council and the primacy. The one church simply cannot have two distinct heads that can be opposed one against the other. A doctrine of episcopal collegiality which might have provided a context within which it would have been possible to harmonize the supreme authority of an ecumenical council with the *plenitudo potestatis* of

---

[10] This is brought out convincingly by C. Moeller, "La collégialité au concile de Constance," in *La collégialité épiscopale* (Paris: Cerf, 1965), 131–49.

the primacy was not present in the ecclesiology of that time. One of the most important lessons from the conciliarist period, therefore, seems to be that collegiality is the congenial framework within which primacy can function within the episcopal body in a way that expresses the evangelical pattern of authority as service and allows all the bishops, together with the head of their college, to cooperate harmoniously with each other.

The Hesitancy of Trent

The period between the end of the Council of Basil-Ferrara-Florence-Rome (1445) and the discussion of the relation between primacy and episcopacy in the closing sessions of the Council of Trent (1562–1563) was characterized by a number of divergent tendencies. On the one hand, the popes gradually were able to reject with increasing force the conciliarist pretensions, culminating in Lateran V's affirmation of the pope's full right and power to convoke, transfer, and dissolve councils (DH 1445). Moreover, the theory of papal supremacy within the church found a powerful expression in John of Torquemada's (1388–1468) *Summa de ecclesia.* In terms of ecclesial structure, "the pope is not a part of the church but the whole; only Peter was made a bishop directly by Christ (II 32–34) and all who enjoy jurisdiction in the Church receive it from the pope (II 54)." Torquemada's role as principal supporter for the restoration of papal primacy was taken up by his fellow Dominican Thomas of Vio (Cajetan; 1469–1534), whose *De comparatione auctoritatis Papae et Concilii* (1511) reaffirms much of Torquemada's teaching. Cajetan proposes a monarchical vision of the papacy. Before the ascension of Christ, all the apostles were of equal power; but after Christ's departure, Peter alone remained as Christ's vicar, and the other apostles received their authority from him, just as the bishops now derive their authority from the pope.[11]

---

[11] Congar, *HDG* III 3d, 38-39. See also Antón, *El misterio de la Igle-*

At the same time, however, the conciliarist view of the church was in no way completely vanquished during this period. The pope had received decisive support in his victory over conciliarism from secular rulers, for which he had to pay by conceding more secular control of the appointment of bishops as well as secular rights to approve the publication of ecclesiastical decrees, concessions that remained in force until the nineteenth century in much of Europe.[12] Those who promoted the conciliar idea would now find refuge in the power of secular rulers and would continue to exert influence in the universities, especially in France, Germany, Italy, and Spain.[13] This continuing vitality of the proponents of episcopal authority helps to explain the otherwise puzzling turn of events at the Council of Trent.

Before turning to those events, a brief word should be said about the affirmation of papal primacy in *Laetentur caeli* (July 6, 1439), the formula for union with the Greek churches from the Council of Florence. This formula affirms that the pope is the successor to Peter and that, as such, he enjoys the *plenitudo potestatis,* which Christ entrusted to Peter to shepherd, rule, and govern the whole church, "just as this is contained in the acts of the ecumenical councils and in the sacred canons" (*quemadmodum etiam in gestis oecumenicorum Conciliorum et in sacris canonibus continetur* [DH 1307]). The decree goes on to "renew" the order, rights, and privileges of the patriarchal churches.

> We also define that the holy apostolic see and the Roman
> pontiff holds the primacy over the whole world and the
> Roman pontiff is the successor of blessed Peter prince of the

---

sia, 1:422–32 and 856–58, the latter commenting on Cajetan's *De divina institutione pontificatus totius Ecclesiae in persona Petri Apostoli* (1521).

[12] So Schatz, *Papal Primacy,* 110–11, who adds that the true victor in the conciliarist controversy was "the established religion of the emerging modern princely states."

[13] Antón provides much information on this continued survival of the conciliarists (*El misterio de la Iglesia,* 1:364–82).

apostles, and that he is the true vicar of Christ, the head of the whole Church and the father and teacher of all Christians and to him was committed in blessed Peter the full power of tending, ruling and governing the whole church, as is contained also in the acts of ecumenical councils and in the sacred canons. Also, renewing the order of the other patriarchs which has been handed down in the canons, the patriarch of Constantinople should be second after the most holy Roman pontiff, third should be the patriarch of Alexandria, fourth the patriarch of Antioch, and fifth the patriarch of Jerusalem, without prejudice to all their privileges and rights.[14]

To be noticed here, first of all, is that the reference to the ecumenical councils and sacred canons can be understood in two different ways: either as a confirmation of papal prerogatives (they were already acknowledged in the revered decisions of the past) or as their limitation (they are restricted to what had been decided in the past). Probably this reference was understood in the first sense by the Latins and in the second sense by the Greeks.

Second, it is interesting to compare Florence's formula of union, which was worked out together with the Greeks, with the profession of faith of Michael Paeleologus, which served as the basis of the attempted union between East and West at the Second Council of Lyon (1274).[15] This latter had not been properly the product of a conciliar discussion between representatives from East and West, but simply had been prepared by the papal curia for the emperor's acceptance. The earlier document contains the statement: "In the Roman Church however rests the fullness of power, such that she admits the other churches to a share in this concern" (*Ad hanc* [the Roman church] *autem sic potestatis plenitudo con-*

---

[14] Tanner, *Decrees of the Ecumenical Councils*, 1:528.

[15] See H. Wolter and H. Holstein, *Lyon I et Lyon II*, "Histoire des conciles 7" (Paris: Ed. de l'Orante, 1966); and J. Gill, *Byzantium and the Papacy 1198–1400* (New Brunswick: Rutgers University Press, 1979), 120–41.

sistit, quod ecclesias ceteras ad sollicitudinis partem admittit
[DH 861]). This suggests that the other churches derive their
power from the church of Rome. The later formula, from
Florence, does not say this. Since the bull of reunion begins
with the name of the reigning pope (*Eugenius episcopus,
servus servorum Dei . . .*), the plural verb *renovantes* (DH
1308), renewing the order of the other patriarchs, could be
interpreted as meaning that the bishop of Rome, using the
majestic "we" form, presents himself as the source of this
order. Whatever the case may be regarding *renovantes*, it
seems undeniable that Florence is more modest than II Lyon
about the dependence of the local churches and their bishops
on the church of Rome and the pope. This will be precisely
one of the issues of controversy at the Council of Trent.

Because of the forceful rejection of papal primacy by a
number of the Protestant Reformers, one reasonably might
have expected that the primacy would have been strongly
reaffirmed by the Council of Trent.[16] But this did not happen.
Some bishops and theologians favored the view, stemming
from Augustinus Triumphus and others that the jurisdiction
of bishops was conferred by the pope. Others, especially the
French and the Spanish, considered episcopal jurisdiction to
be conferred directly by Christ. These opposing groups—
within the body of Catholic bishops at the council, it should
be remembered—also differed on the question of the necessity of episcopal residence. The former group claimed that the
pope enjoys the power to dispense individual bishops from
the normal duty of residing in the dioceses which they lead;
the latter objected that the intimate relation binding together
the bishop and the local church is *iure divino*, established by
Christ himself, in such a way that even the pope has no
authority to alter this essential structure. The bishops were

---

[16] An extensive presentation of the discussions at Trent is G. Alberigo's
"Le potestà episcopali secondo i padri del concilio di Trento," the first
chapter of his *Lo sviluppo della dottrina sui poteri nella chiesa universale*
(Rome: Herder, 1964), 11–101.

so evenly and sharply divided over these issues that the papal legates presiding at the council were instructed to guide the discussion away from any decision about papal primacy and its relation to the institution and jurisdiction of the episcopacy.[17]

It would seem that at least two conclusions emerge from this period that have relevance for the relation between primacy and episcopacy. First of all, the position that would separate the two terms or even give the episcopacy, when gathered in council, a certain primacy over the bishop of Rome, does not seem to sufficiently preserve that freedom from subordination to a superior instance of authority without which the primacy would lose its meaningfulness. If it is Christ's will that there should be a personal, primatial ministry that has the effective authority to serve the overall unity of the church, ultimately such a primacy should not be subordinated to a higher court of appeal. That being said, this period, which includes not only the Great Western Schism with three competing popes but also the oftentimes scandalous Renaissance papacy, shows that the primacy is in no way immune from weakness and failure. What remedy can be found for such deficiencies? Perhaps one can be found in the steadfast practice of episcopal collegiality. If the whole body of bishops collaborate with a genuinely fraternal and collegial spirit, then the bishop of Rome could find the conditions needed to fully exercise his primatial responsibility of serving unity, while at the same time be also the recipient of such assistance as he may need from the other bishops, including the most precious, and most difficult to bestow, gift of fraternal correction. Second, this period shows that the view that all authority and jurisdiction flow from the

---

[17] See James Puglisi, *Étude comparative sur les processus d'acces au ministère ordonné*, Tome III/1 (diss., Paris: Institut catholique, 1991), 703–4, with citation and bibliography concerning the letter of June 26, 1563, of Cardinal Borromeo to the papal legates at Trent. See also G. Dejaifve, "Les douze apôtres et leur unité dans la tradition catholique," *Ephemerides Theologicae Lovanienses* 39 (1963): 773–74.

pope was not able to gain conciliar ratification, even as late
as the Council of Trent and after the forceful expositions of
so many proponents of the papacy during the many centuries that followed the Gregorian reform. In its own way,
Vatican I, while defining papal primacy, would also refrain
from embracing the more absolutist theories of papal
authority.

CHAPTER 7

The Struggle over Authority:
Trent to Vatican I

The period after Trent gave birth to the Catholic theology of the Counter-Reformation. It would be unfair to judge Robert Bellarmine's *De controversiis Christianae Fidei adversus huius temporis haereticos* (Concerning the controversies of the Christian faith against the heretics of these times, 1586–1593) as limiting the church to its visible and hierarchical dimensions.[1] Though he claimed that the church was as visible "as the Republic of Venice," he did not ignore the spiritual, graced reality of the church as the body of Christ. Nevertheless, his apologetic against the ecclesiology of the Protestant Reformers led Bellarmine (1542–1621) to emphasize the church's external qualities and even to see the notes of the church from the creed (unity, holiness, catholicity, and apostolicity, to which he added many other distinguishing traits) as obvious to any observer. One need not have faith to know which was the true church of Christ; it could be demonstrated from observation and reason. Christ is head of the church, and the pope, as Christ's vicar, enjoys the supreme power of jurisdiction that comes to him through succession to the Petrine ministry. His full pastoral power extends over all the faithful and their pastors. Following the doctrine of Torquemada and Cajetan, Bellarmine sees in the

---

[1] Contained in his *Opera omnia* (Paris: L. Vivès, 1870–74), vols. 1–7. For our theme, see B. de Margerie, "Jésus, Pierre et les Douze suivant Bellarmin," *Sciences ecclésiastiques* 18 (1966): 371–93.

pope the center and source of all ecclesial power. The church has a monarchical structure under the headship of Christ the King; the pope and bishops serve as instruments of this headship. But because Bellarmine recognizes that the episcopacy was also established by Christ (*ius divinum*), the structure of the church on earth (*ecclesia militans*) is not purely monarchical. The bishops are not mere delegates of the pope.

Concerning the distinction between order and jurisdiction, Bellarmine acknowledges the divine origin of the power of orders but maintains that, while the apostles received their jurisdiction immediately from Christ, the bishops receive it by mediation through the pope, thus reinforcing the unity of the church as a whole. Moreover, while he acknowledges the full and immediate power of the individual bishop in his diocese, Bellarmine gives even greater attention to the "collegial" action of bishops gathered in ecumenical councils, which are the ordinary means to resolve grave crises. His ecclesiology gives a great deal of attention to the ecumenical councils; it is from him that the Roman church draws its criteria for numbering these councils and so considers Vatican II to be the twenty-first in the series. In summary, Bellarmine relates the primacy and the episcopacy in such a way as to affirm the divine origin of each, to subordinate the latter to the former and to see in that subordination no denigration of the episcopacy.

The position of Bellarmine's fellow Jesuit and contemporary Francisco Suárez (1548–1617) seems quite similar. Arguing against the Protestants, he categorically affirms the necessity of the episcopacy: "in no way can a true church exist without a bishop" (*vera autem ecclesia sine episcopo esse nullo modo potest*).[2] At the same time, he makes the

---

[2] Francisco Suárez, *Comm. in II^a II^{ae}, disp. IX De ecclesia*, sect. IX n. 10, in *Opera omnia*, ed. L. Vivès (Paris: 1856–78), 12:278. On Suárez's view of the relation between the pope and the bishops, indicating the subtlety and, at times, inconsistency of his position, see G. Alberigo, *Lo*

bishops radically dependent on the pope by sharply differentiating the powers of order and jurisdiction in such a way that the latter in no way derives from episcopal consecration.[3] Thus all episcopal power of jurisdiction derives from its being granted by the pope.

Accentuating the Role of the Bishops

This emphasis on central authority was put into practice by the popes of the time, who tended to be strong leaders in directing the Catholic reformation after Trent. Nevertheless, various factors led to a renewed interest in the episcopacy during the seventeenth and eighteenth centuries. First of all, the period after Trent saw a decline in the prestige and authority of the college of cardinals, especially in the rejection of the view, dominant at the time of the Council of Constance, that the college of cardinals was an institution established by Christ himself and was thus "by divine decree" (*iure divino*).[4] It followed logically that, when theologians now would consider the "collegial" nature of the church, their attention would focus not upon the cardinals but upon the bishops. Most of all, however, increased reflection about the episcopacy was sparked by several new ecclesiologies which blended an emphasis on the authority of the bishops with a certain nationalistic spirit. These came to be

---

sviluppo della dottrina sui poteri nella chiesa universale (Rome: Herder, 1964), 179–207.

[3] For example: "*in episcopo nullus est actus iurisdictionis qui per se pendeat a consecratione*" (in the bishop nothing of the act of jurisdiction of its nature comes from consecration) and "*character, seu consecratio episcopalis non est principium per se alicuius actus iurisdictionis*" (character, or episcopal consecration, is not of its nature the basis of any act of jurisdiction). See *De legibus* book 4, chapter 4, n. 9; in *Opera omnia*, 5:342.

[4] Alberigo, *Lo sviluppo*, 106–9. See also idem, "La collégialité épiscopale selon quelques théologiens de la papauté," in *La collégialité épiscopale* (Paris: Cerf, 1965), 183–221, at 196.

known by the names Gallicanism, Febronianism, Josephism, and episcopalism.

In 1611, E. Richer (1559–1631), the editor of the works of the conciliarists Peter of Ailly and John Gerson, wrote his *De ecclesiastica et politica potestate*. He passionately opposed the view that the church can be understood simply from the perspective of the pope as its hierarchical summit. The power of the keys was given to the church as a whole. The pope is its ministerial head; the church delegates its power to him. Richer's views found wide acceptance in France, in part because of their appeal to the French kings. J.-B. Bossuet espoused a Gallicanism in which the apostles all received directly from Christ the same episcopal power.[5] This power was first given to Peter, as head of the body of bishops, so that his successor, the pope, would enjoy the fullness of power which the other individual bishops enjoyed within the confines of their single local churches. But the power of the bishops does not come from the pope. It has its own proper origin and, for this reason, the consent of the bishops is necessary in order that any papal decision have binding force for the whole church.

Bossuet was the author of the four "Gallican Articles" promulgated by the Assembly of the Clergy of France on March 19, 1682.[6] Article 1 affirmed the independence of the king in secular affairs. Article 2 acknowledged that the successors of Peter, as vicars of Christ, enjoy full authority in spiritual matters, but also professed allegiance to the statements about the authority of ecumenical councils from the Council of Constance. Article 3 affirmed that the exercise of apostolic authority must be moderated by the canons that

---

[5] See A. G. Martimort, *Le Gallicanisme de Bossuet* (Paris: Cerf, 1953).

[6] The Gallican Articles are reprinted in English in appendix 6 of K. Schatz, *Papal Primacy: From Its Origins to the Present* (Collegeville, Minn.: Liturgical Press, 1996), 188–89. Their condemnation by Alexander III in 1690 can be found in DH 2281–84.

had been established in antiquity with the assistance of the Holy Spirit and accepted throughout the world, and that the rules, usages, and institutions established in France lose none of their force because of the pope's authority. Finally, article 4 admits that the pope is the superior guide in matters of faith, but it asserts that his judgments are not immutable without the approval of the church. These ideas became the required doctrine in French seminaries and gained wide acceptance in parts of Germany, Italy, and the United States.

The Gallicans were convinced that theirs was the more original view of ecclesial order, which went back to the ancient church and thus to before the imposition of a theocratic ecclesiology by Pseudo-Isidore, Gregory VII, the decretalists, and the scholastic theologians. This conviction was shared by J. N. Hontheim (1701–1790), who, under the pseudonym Febronius, published his *De statu ecclesiae et legitima potestate Romani Pontificis* in 1763.[7] Febronius simply develops the ideas of his French predecessors. The church as a whole has the power of the keys and exercises this through its ministers. The role of the pope is to maintain unity by the service of vigilance and exhortation; his primacy is that of a *primus inter pares*. The bishops receive their power immediately from Jesus Christ and govern their dioceses independently, that is, bound only by the scriptures, the canons of the ecumenical councils and the obligation to act for the good of the faithful.[8] They must recover the rights inherent in their task, which the Holy See has unjustly taken away. Many of these ideas also filtered into Italy in the

---

[7] Febronius's epitaph in this regard is revealing: *Ecclesiam Christi ad primaevum revocans statum legitimos potestati Romani Pontificis assignavit limites* ("Recalling the church of Christ to its primeval state he assigned legitimate limits to the power of the Roman pontiff"). Cited in G. Dejaifve, "Les douze apôtres et leur unité dans la tradition catholique," in *L'Épiscopat et l'Église universelle* (Paris: Cerf, 1962), 777.

[8] So Angel Antón, *El misterio de la Iglesia* (Madrid/Toledo: BAC, 1986, 1987), 2:107.

works of such theologians as Pietro Tamburini (1737–1827; *La vera idea della Santa Sede* [1784]) and in the doctrines of the Synod of Pistoia of 1786.[9]

This promotion of the authority of the episcopacy led, in the late 1700s, to efforts on the part of theologians favorable to the papacy to develop an ecclesiology which better harmonized the primacy with the episcopacy. One who is widely praised by historians of ecclesiology for doing this is M. Gerbert (1720–1793), whose *De communione potestatis ecclesiasticae inter summos ecclesiae principes pontificem, et episcopos* (On the communion of ecclesiastical power between the highest princes of the church, the pontiff, and the bishops) was published in 1761.[10] For Gerbert, categories drawn from the legal structures of secular society can never be sufficient to express the reality of the church, for they place in competition what should harmoniously work together. Only by seeing that the church is a communion can one understand that there need be no opposition between primacy and episcopacy. Gerbert's principal thesis is that the relation between primacy and episcopacy is analogous to that between Peter and the apostles in the apostolic college. The episcopal college succeeds to the college of the apostles. The powers given to Peter personally and individually were communicated, in a second moment, to the college of apostles as a whole, to be exercised collegially. The pope cannot be isolated from the college, since he is a member of it; but he is a member *sui generis*, as the college's head. While there can be tensions and difficulties between the pope and the

---

[9] Some of the errors of the Synod of Pistoia, condemned by Pius VI in 1794 (e.g., DH 2602–15), derive from the Gallicanism of Richer and Febronius. So Congar, *HDG* III 3d, 79.

[10] For an extensive and laudatory exposition of Gerbert's ecclesiology, see Alberigo, *Lo sviluppo*, 226–56. Appreciative comments can also be found in Antón, *El misterio de la Iglesia*, 2:111–13; Congar *HDG* III 3d, 73–74; and G. Dejaifve, "La collegialità nella tradizione latina," in *La Chiesa del Vaticano II*, ed. G. Baraúna (Florence: Vallecchi, 1965), 848.

bishops, these can be resolved by working together. Thus, not an abstract principle of power but rather the reality and practice of communion are the solution to the tension between primacy and episcopacy.

Gerbert's affirmation of papal primacy against Gallicanism and Febronianism within the context of an appreciation of the ministry of episcopacy is expressed by other writers of this period as well. For the Dominican E. D. Cristianopulo (*Della nullità delle assoluzioni nei casi riservati* [On the nullity of absolutions in reserved cases], 1785), secular models of government cannot express that supernatural form of unity which Christ established in the church. Christ instituted a primacy of jurisdiction by virtue of which each bishop depends on the pope as the center of unity in the church. At the same time, the primate functions as head of the bishops in such a way that all the bishops together form one, indivisible episcopate to which the government of the whole church is confided. It is a question of two subjects, inadequately distinct, with the second subject necessarily including the first.[11] P. Ballerini (1698–1769) begins his *De vi ac ratione primatus Romanorum Pontificum* (On the power and basis of the primacy of the Roman pontiffs; 1766) with two chapters proposing the theology of communion as the premise and norm for ecclesial unity and for the primacy of the pope.[12] The pope is the middle point of the communion and the principle of unity. The bishops in ecumenical council have their authority directly from Christ. G. V. Bolgeni, S.J. (1733–1811; *L'episcopato ossia della potestà di governar la Chiesa* [The episcopacy or of the power to govern the church; 1789]) makes Cyprian of Carthage's idea of the unity of the episcopate the central thesis of his doctrine of episcopacy. The unity of the episcopate is conceived in analogy with the unity of the Trinity, in

---

[11] So Antón, *El misterio de la Iglesia*, 2:115.
[12] So Alberigo, *Lo sviluppo*, 289.

which the divine essence is one and communicates itself to the Son and the Spirit. In an analogous way, there must be a principle, origin, and source of the episcopacy which communicates itself to the other bishops. This visible source is the pope as successor to Peter.[13] Within this monarchical view of the papacy in which the bishops can even be spoken of as vicars to the pope, Bolgeni nevertheless speaks of the *ius divinum* of the episcopacy; they have a jurisdiction that is not simply delegated. The episcopal college, together with its head, receives a universal jurisdiction which originally Peter and the apostles received from Christ. The college is the subject of full and universal power together with its head, the pope, and never separated from him. In this sense, Bolgeni distinguishes between two kinds of jurisdiction: the universal jurisdiction of the college of bishops, which its members possess *iure divino* in virtue of episcopal consecration and the particular or territorial jurisdiction which is conferred by the pope.[14]

By 1800, the papacy seemed to have reached its lowest point in the modern era. Pius VI died the previous year at Valence, a prisoner of Napoleon. Many French and German theologians were convinced that the papal system and, particularly, papal infallibility, had been overcome and were now of merely historical interest. And yet the French Revolution and subsequent events led to a popular reawakening of interest in papal authority which blossomed into the Ultramontanism that characterized the second third of the nineteenth century, under the inspiration of such writers as J. De Maistre (1753–1827), whose *Du pape* of 1819 seemed to root all hope for society ultimately in the authority and even infallibility of the pope. Within this movement of the restoration of the papacy must be situated Vatican I, with its definitions about papal primacy and infallibility.

---

[13] So *L'episcopato*, 1.6, n. 76; in Alberigo, *Lo sviluppo*, 326–27.
[14] So Congar, *HDG* III 3d, 74–75.

The First Vatican Council

S. Boulgakov, in 1929, likened the action of the Roman Catholic bishops at Vatican I to "collective suicide."[15] However, various studies of the process that led to the final texts promulgated by the council show that this was far from the case.[16] The preparatory draft for a constitution *De Ecclesiae constitutione* included two chapters (11–12) that treated papal primacy; these were based on *vota* that had been prepared by P. Cossa, F. Hettinger, and G. Perrone and had been synthesized into an eight-page summary by C. Schrader.[17]

---

[15] S. Boulgakov, "Le dogme du Vatican," French translation from the original Russian printed in *Le messager orthodoxe* 6 (1960): 25. Cited in G. Dejaifve, "Primauté et collégialité au premier concile du Vatican," in *L'Épiscopat et l'Église universelle* (Paris: Cerf, 1962), 639.

[16] The bibliography on Vatican I is vast. Some titles relevant to the council's doctrine of episcopacy include C. Colombo, "Il problema dell'episcopato nella Costituzione 'De Ecclesia catholica' del Concilio Vaticano I," *La Scuola Cattolica* 89 (1961): 344–72; G. Dejaifve, *Pape et évêques au premier concile du Vatican* (Bruges: Desclée de Brouwer, 1961); W. F. Dewan, "*Potestas vere episcopalis* au premier Concile du Vatican," in *De Doctrina Concilii Vaticani Primi* (Vatican City: Libreria Editrice Vaticana, 1969), 661–87; J. Hamer, "Le corps épiscopal uni au pape, son autorité dans l'Eglise, d'après les documents du I concile du Vatican," *Revue des sciences philosophiques et théologiques* 45 (1961): 21–31; W. Kasper, "Primat und Episkopat nach dem Vatikanum I," *Tübinger theologische Quartalschrift* 142 (1962): 47–83; H. J. Pottmeyer, *Toward a Papacy in Communion: Perspectives from Vatican Councils I and II* (New York: Crossroad, 1998); J. P. Torrell, *La théologie de l'épiscopat au premier concile du Vatican* (Paris: Cerf, 1961).

[17] These all agreed that papal primacy should be defined as episcopal; as extending over the whole church, including bishops and ecumenical councils; as having an authority that is full, supreme, ordinary, and immediate; as having the right to convoke, preside over, and confirm councils, to appoint, depose, and transfer bishops, to make laws applicable to the universal church, to judge *causae maiores*, to exercise authority anywhere and at any time, and to be free of control by civil authorities in publishing and applying decrees. On the drafts, see R. Minnerath, *Le pape évêque universel ou premier des évêques?* (Paris: Beauchesne, 1978), 11–37; and

Concern about the proper relation between primacy and episcopacy emerged in the observations made by the bishops about chapter 11.[18] Here one finds a sharp criticism of any teaching about the primacy that would not mention its relation to the ordinary power and jurisdiction of the bishops, thus isolating it from its proper context.[19] Bishop Melchers of Cologne summarized the sentiments of many bishops when he wrote: "one would hope for a presentation of the bishops as successors to the apostles, without which the true notion of the primacy and its raison d'être within the hierarchy can be neither understood nor well presented."[20] This concern became even more acute when it was decided to treat the material about papal primacy in a separate "first constitution" on the church, which would become *Pastor aeternus*, leaving the material about the church as a whole to be dealt with in a later document.

The discussion of the draft of *Pastor aeternus* itself further brought out the need to safeguard the legitimate authority of the bishops, particularly in connection with the affirmation of the second paragraph of chapter 3, which states that "the Roman Church holds the pre-eminence of ordinary power over all the other Churches; and that this power of jurisdiction of the Roman Pontiff, which is truly episcopal, is immediate" (DH 3060).[21] Some criticized the use of the word

---

G. Thils, *Primauté et infaillibilité du pontife romain à Vatican I* (Leuven: University Press, 1989), 15–40. Thils shows that the notes used in these preliminary studies clearly demonstrate that their presentations of papal primacy were directed against the errors of various Gallicans and Jansenists (pp. 24ff.).

[18] See Mansi 51:929–68.

[19] So Bishops Schwarzenberg (Mansi 51:930D); Fürstenberg (932D); Tarnoczy (935B–C); Haynald (937C); Krementz (948C); Moreno (949C); and Jirsik (965A). See U. Betti, *La costituzione dommatica "Pastor aeternus" del Concilio Vaticano I* (Rome: Pontificio Ateneo Antonianum, 1961), 181–91.

[20] Mansi 51:936A.

[21] The problem with the adjectives "episcopal," "ordinary," and "immediate" is carefully presented by T. I. Jimenez-Urresti, "L'autorité du

"ordinary" in that it seemed to imply either two competing jurisdictions within any one diocese or that the local bishop would be merely a vicar of the pope.[22] Others challenged the use of the word "episcopal," saying that a papal intervention in a diocese other than his own is due to his primacy, not to the fact that he is a bishop.[23] Bishops Doupanloup, Strossmayer, and Haynald all recalled Gregory the Great's rejection of the title "universal bishop" on the grounds that such a title would effectively diminish the episcopal dignity of all the other bishops.[24]

Bishop Zinelli attempted to respond to all of the objections in his important *relatio* on behalf of the theological commission on July 5, 1870.[25] He insisted that the power of papal primacy must be described as episcopal, insofar as it is part of the properly *pastoral* ministry which the pope exercises as a bishop along with the other bishops. He acknowledged that there are two subjects of supreme power in the church—that of the bishops together with the pope and that of the pope alone. Thus two options are excluded: that only the pope enjoys such power and that the pope enjoys such power only when he acts together with the bishops.[26] To appease those who had objections about the statement concerning the episcopal, ordinary, and immediate power of the pope, a further paragraph was added to the text of chapter 3 of *Pastor aeternus*, stating that "the bishops . . . under appointment of the Holy Spirit (cf. Acts 20:28) succeeded in

---

pontife romain sur le collège épiscopal, et, par son intermédiaire, sur l'Église universelle," in *La collégialité épiscopal*, 243–64.

[22] Mansi 51:934D–935A, 957B, 970A. In commenting on the terms "ordinary and immediate," many interventions reaffirmed the ordinary powers of the bishops: see Mansi 51:941D, 955A, 958A, 960D, 965A, and 967D–968A.

[23] So Haynald in Mansi 52:668C–D.

[24] Mansi 52:574B–C, 393A, and 666D.

[25] Mansi 52:1108D–1110C.

[26] Mansi 52:1109C; see also Minnerath, *Le pape évêque universel ou premier des évêques?* 97.

the place of the apostles" (thus by divine institution) and
that the Roman pontiff's power is far from standing in the
way of the ordinary and immediate jurisdictional power of
the bishops (DH 3061). This paragraph also quotes the letter of Gregory the Great about his will to guard the dignity
of his brother bishops, to which various bishops had referred
in their interventions before the council. Bishop D'Avanzo,
on behalf of the theological commission, even acknowledged
certain limits to papal power: according to the will of Christ
this power can only be used to build up and not to harm the
church and the pope must not bypass the bishops, whose
ministry is also divinely instituted for the service of the
church.[27]

In the end, by acknowledging this divine institution of the
ministry of bishops, Vatican I may be said to have sown the
seeds of episcopal collegiality, which would come to fruition
eventually at Vatican II.[28] Moreover, the council refrained
from adopting the view, proposed by so many theologians
since the emergence of the distinction between order and
jurisdiction, that the jurisdiction of the bishops flows from
the primacy as from its source.[29] While much of its acknowledgment of the authority of bishops is implicit and can only
be known by perusal of the acts of the council, nevertheless
this acknowledgment is present.[30] This is demonstrated by

---

[27] Mansi 52:715B–C.

[28] Minnerath, *Le pape évêque universel ou premier des évêques?* 88–
89. Y. Congar comments that various points that were acknowledged by
the theological commission at Vatican I found explicit expression in the
documents of Vatican II ("Il problema ecclesiologico del papato il Vaticano II," in *Ministeri e comunione ecclesiale* [Bologna: Edizioni Dehoniane, 1973], 151).

[29] So Y. Congar, "La collegialità dell' episcopato e il primato del vescovo
di Roma nella storia," in *Ministeri e comunione ecclesiale* (Bologna:
Edizioni Dehoniane, 1973), 103, citing Zinelli's intervention of July 16,
1870, in Mansi 52:1314. See also Minnerath, *Le pape évêque universel ou
premier des évêques?*, 103; and Dejaifve, "Le premier des évêques," 572
n. 31.

[30] Congar remarks that the responses by the theological commission to

the collective declaration of the German bishops in 1875, which received the full approval of Pius IX, in response to a circular of the German chancellor Bismark, who interpreted Vatican I as degrading bishops to the level of mere officials of the pope:

> It is in virtue of the same divine institution upon which the papacy rests that the episcopacy also exists. It, too, has its rights and duties, because of the ordinance of God himself, and the Pope has neither the right nor the power to change them. Thus it is a complete misunderstanding of the Vatican decrees to believe that because of them "episcopal jurisdiction has been absorbed into the papal," that the Pope has "in principle taken the place of each individual bishop," that the bishops are now "no more than tools of the Pope, his officials, without responsibility of their own." According to the constant teaching of the Catholic Church, expressly declared at the Vatican Council itself, the bishops are not mere tools of the Pope, nor papal officials without responsibility of their own, but, "under appointment of the Holy Spirit, they succeeded in the place of the apostles, and feed and rule individually, as true shepherds, the particular flock assigned to them. (DH 3115)

Vatican I may be said to have brought an end, as far as acceptable Catholic teaching is concerned, to several episcopalist doctrines that had emerged and persisted throughout the second millennium in reaction to the general tendency to affirm papal primacy. Chief among these doctrines were (1) the conciliarist position that the subjection of the primate to the decision of an ecumenical council is compatible with the affirmation of papal primacy and (2) the Gallican posi-

---

the objections raised by the bishops often conceded the truth of those objections ("Il problema ecclesiologico del papato dopo Vaticano II," 150–51). But in order to avoid any semblance of placing Gallican limitations on papal primacy, these concessions were not explicitly incorporated into the final text of *Pastor aeternus*. See also Dejaifve, "Le premier des évêques," 570.

tion that the primate's ministry of promoting the health of the communion as a whole can only be exercised on the condition of the approbation of the local churches.[31] At the same time, by explicitly acknowledging the divine institution of the episcopacy and by affirming that the primacy in no way detracts from the authority of bishops, Vatican I may equally be said to have brought an end to the more absolutist theories of papal primacy and paved the way for Vatican II.[32]

---

[31] Both the historical context and the actual text of *Pastor aeternus* show that the latter, Gallican position was the principal doctrine excluded by Vatican I. Nevertheless, the statement in DH 3063—"Therefore, those who say that it is permitted to appeal to an ecumenical Council from the decisions of the Roman Pontiff, as to an authority superior to the Roman Pontiff, are far from the straight path of truth"—shows that Vatican I has implications also with regard to the earlier conciliarist doctrine.

[32] Antón writes: "It is correct . . . to assert with J. Ratzinger that the studies about Vatican I in the last few decades have demonstrated 'that, according to Vatican I not only episcopalism but also papalism, in its strict sense, must be considered as abolished doctrines'" (*El misterio de la Iglesia*, 2:366–67). The quotation from Ratzinger is taken from K. Rahner and J. Ratzinger, *Episkopat und Primat* (Freiburg: Herder, 1961), 43. W. Kasper provides a list of theologians who share this judgment ("Primat und Episkopat nach dem Vatikanum I," 48, nn. 4 and 5).

Chapter 8

Vatican II: Communion, Collegiality, and Primacy

The ninety years extending from the opening of Vatican I to the announcement of Vatican II constitute a period of immense theological ferment, which included not only the tensions surrounding biblical criticism, modernism, and the "*nouvelle théologie*" but also a vigorous "return to the sources." Historical methods applied to these sources provided a wealth of new insights about scripture, liturgy, patristic literature, and the histories of dogma and of theology itself. The precise theme of the relation between primacy and episcopacy was not the focus of most of this research, although, indirectly, such a return to the sources allowed theologians to become more familiar with the nature of the episcopacy and the development of the primacy in the early centuries of the life of the church. The principal ecclesiological advances of the twentieth century concerned such themes as the Mystical Body of Christ, the people of God and the church as fundamental sacrament. These brought fresh ideas to the understanding of the church as a whole, but did not, in themselves, occasion a deeper reflection about the relation between primacy and episcopacy.[1] It was rather John XXIII's

---

[1] See Angel Antón, *El misterio de la Iglesia* (Madrid/Toledo: BAC, 1986, 1987), 2:542–58 and 612–653 (on the Mystical Body), 676–759 (on the people of God), and 760–831 (on the church as sacrament). In Antón's extensive presentation of these themes, there is relatively little about the topic of primacy and episcopacy.

143

convocation of a council, with its intention to focus on the nature of the church and to bring to completion the work of Vatican I, which really provided the impetus for increased attention to our theme.

The Sacramentality of the Episcopacy

Without making the mistake of completely opposing the two views, it can scarcely be doubted that Vatican II constituted a shift from viewing the church predominantly in terms of its societal and juridical structure to considering it fundamentally in its sacramental, ontological reality.[2] This shift in perspective was in many ways the fruit of the historical *ressourcement* and of the ecclesiological developments mentioned in the previous paragraph. In addition, this shift had a profound effect on the council's doctrine of the episcopacy and its relation to the primacy. Yves Congar wrote that "the only passage of the Dogmatic Constitution on the Church which could be considered as a true and proper dogmatic declaration is that which concerns the sacramentality of the episcopacy (Chap. III, n. 21). It resolves, in fact, a question which up until now had been a matter of free discussion among theologians."[3] The crucial passage reads:

> In order to fulfill such exalted functions, the apostles were endowed by Christ with a special outpouring of the Holy Spirit coming upon them (cf. Acts 1:8; 2:4; John 20:22–23),

---

[2] This was the conclusion of Y. Congar in the final sections of his published diary of the council, *Le concile au jour le jour: Quatrième session* (Paris: Cerf, 1966), 119–52, especially 128–30.

[3] Y. Congar, "In luogo di conclusione," in *La Chiesa del Vaticano II*, ed. G. Baraúna (Florence: Vallecchi, 1965), 1262 (hereafter, Baraúna). See also J. Lécuyer, "L'Episcopato come sacramento," in Baraúna, 713–32, who concludes: "In the Constitution on the Church, in many ways so rich and so new, the few lines about the sacramentality of the episcopate could seem to be rather secondary. In fact, I believe that they are fundamental and that the theology of the Church in the coming years will uncover their importance more and more."

and, by the imposition of hands (cf. 1 Tim. 4:14; 2 Tim. 1:6–7), they passed on to their auxiliaries the gift of the Spirit, which is transmitted down to our day through episcopal consecration. The holy Synod teaches, moreover, that the fullness of the sacrament of Orders is conferred by episcopal consecration, that fullness, namely, which both in the liturgical tradition of the Church and in the language of the Fathers of the Church is called the high priesthood, the acme of the sacred ministry. Now, episcopal consecration confers, together with the office of sanctifying, the office also of teaching and ruling, which, however, of their very nature can be exercised only in hierarchical communion with the head and members of the college. (*Lumen gentium* 21)

What one should notice here, first of all, is that the episcopacy, with its three offices (*munera*) of teaching, sanctifying, and governing, is said to be rooted in the sacrament of episcopal consecration. The view sometimes held by Thomas Aquinas and by other scholastic theologians that there was no sacramental difference between a priest and a bishop is excluded.[4] In this way, Vatican II went against a conception of ordained ministry that had greatly influenced the way in which many Catholic theologians had understood the relation between episcopacy and primacy over the course of the second millennium. If ordination is considered mainly as conferring the power to celebrate the Eucharist and the other sacraments, then the precise difference between the bishop and the priest is to be located not in the power of orders as such, which they share, but in something else, the power of jurisdiction, which is granted to the individual bishop by the pope when he is assigned a portion of the flock to teach and

---

[4] For a brief explanation of this scholastic opinion, see Y. Congar, *HDG* III 3c, 154; and J. Ratzinger, "La collegialità episcopale dal punto di vista teologico," in Baraúna, 739–40. For Aquinas, see J. Lécuyer, "Les étapes de l'enseignement thomiste sur l'épiscopat," *Revue Thomiste* 57 (1957): 29–52. For the discussion of the relation between the episcopacy and the presbyterate at the Council of Trent, see Antón, *Il misterio de la Iglesia*, 1:732–38.

to shepherd. Such a view tended to weaken the sacramental foundation of episcopal ministry and to heighten the bishop's dependence on the pope. One of the fruits of the renewal in liturgical and patristic studies during the first decades of the twentieth century had been to make even clearer the fundamental sacramentality of the episcopal ministry. If too much weight is placed on the distinction between order and jurisdiction, the bond between the sacramental ordination of the bishop and his mission to shepherd his flock can be weakened. The mission of the bishop to shepherd a local church could then appear so dependent on his receiving jurisdiction that the sacramental basis of the episcopacy, so evident in the liturgies of the episcopal ordination that have come down to us from the patristic era, seems to be neglected.[5] By identifying episcopal consecration as the source of the three offices of sanctifying, teaching, and governing, *Lumen gentium* 21 avoids this danger and even suggests that the distinction between the powers of order and of jurisdiction is perhaps not as sharp as has sometimes been believed.[6] One thing is sure, the council clearly rejected the view that the primary, distinguishing mark of the episcopacy is to be found in the power of jurisdiction.

However, the same text also affirms that, of their very nature, the three *munera* "can be exercised only in hierarchical communion with the head and members of the college." Thus the exercise of the sacramentally based offices of the

---

[5] See, for example, the rich contribution by the canons regular of Mondaye about the meaning of the ministry of the bishop as woven into fourteen different early liturgies for episcopal consecration: "Évêque d'après les prières d'ordination," in *L'Episcopat et l'Église universelle* (Paris: Cerf, 1962), 739–80.

[6] Commenting on this text, J. Ratzinger writes: "The sharp distinction between the power of order and the power of jurisdiction, which had for centuries been introduced in the thought of the larger part of western theologians, now is made more fluid, and the intimate connection of the two realities which, in the ultimate analysis, constitute one sole thing, appears clear before the eyes" ("La collegialità episcopale dal punto di visto teologico," 737).

bishop should be situated within the context of a college, comprised of head and members. This becomes especially clear when we look at the sequence of topics treated in the crucial paragraphs of *Lumen gentium* about the bishops. Paragraph 21 is placed between other paragraphs that speak, first, of the origin and then of the exercise of episcopal ministry. The two paragraphs about the origin of the episcopal college parallel exactly the first two chapters of Vatican I's *Pastor aeternus*. Just as chapter 1 of *Pastor aeternus* describes the divine institution of the primacy of Peter, so *Lumen gentium* 19 describes the divine institution of the college of the apostles. Just as chapter 2 of *Pastor aeternus* teaches that the bishop of Rome is successor to Peter in the ministry of the primacy, so *Lumen gentium* 20 teaches that the college of bishops is successor to the college of the apostles.

The three paragraphs that then follow *Lumen gentium* 21 explore important characteristics of the college. Paragraph 22 speaks of the relation of the head and members, making two references to the explanations given by Bishop Zinelli at Vatican I. Here we find the important affirmation: "Together with their head, the Supreme Pontiff, and never apart from him, they [the bishops] have supreme and full authority over the universal Church; but this power cannot be exercised without the agreement of the Roman Pontiff." Paragraph 23 discusses the relations between the bishops, adding that just as the pope serves as the visible principle of unity for the whole church so do the bishops serve as visible principles of unity for each local church. Finally, paragraph 24 describes the exercise of episcopal ministry, a ministry of service (*diakonia*) received from the Lord and empowered by the Holy Spirit. One should understand the reference here to the "canonical mission" of the bishops as a further specification of that "hierarchical communion" spoken of earlier in *Lumen gentium* 21. The expression "canonical mission" preserves within Vatican II's vision of episcopal ministry the importance of and need for the granting of jurisdiction. What should not be overlooked, however, is the affirmation that this canonical mission "can be made by legitimate customs that have not been revoked by the supreme and universal authority of the Church, or by laws made or acknowledged by the same authority." To this is appended a note referring to the canon law of the Oriental Catholic churches. This implies that the "granting of canonical mission" can be understood in a variety of ways, including those ways from the ancient traditions of the first millennium, by which the bishops of Rome acknowledged the mission of bishops of the Eastern patriarchates. Thus the forms of granting jurisdiction that were developed only in the West and, in some cases, in more recent centuries, need not be the only ways in which "hierarchical communion" be maintained. These considerations concerning especially the structure of *Lumen gentium* 19–24 clearly show that the episcopal college is the framework within which Vatican II understands not only the sacramental nature of the episcopacy but also the relation between the episcopacy and the primacy of the pope.

It is well known that on October 30, 1963, a decisive vote was taken at Vatican II concerning the question of whether the Constitution on the Church should frame the discussion of the episcopacy within the context of the *college* of bishops.[7] The very notion of collegiality was problematic for a minority of the bishops, who did not understand it as being compatible with what Vatican I had defined regarding papal primacy. As the text emerged, *Lumen gentium* 22 turned out to be the principal paragraph that described the episcopal college.

---

[7] Some objected to the validity of such a vote, since it concerned not the approval of the text of a particular draft, as such, but rather the general orientation that the subsequent drafts should take. One of the most authoritative sources for information about Vatican II's Constitution on the Church, G. Philips, gives a brief account of this event in his "History of the Constitution [*Lumen gentium*]," in H. Vorgrimler, *Commentary on the Documents of Vatican II* (London: Burns & Oates, 1967), 1:105–37, at 115–18.

Just as, in accordance with the Lord's decree, St. Peter and the rest of the apostles constitute a unique apostolic college, so in like fashion the Roman Pontiff, Peter's successor, and the bishops, the successors of the apostles, are related with and united to one another. (*Lumen gentium* 22)

The *unity* of the college provides the key for Vatican II's understanding of the relation between primacy and episcopacy: "In order that the episcopate itself, however, might be one and undivided he [Christ] put Peter at the head of the other apostles, and in him he set up a lasting and visible source and foundation of the unity both of faith and of communion" (*Lumen gentium* 18). Or again: "The Roman Pontiff, as the successor of Peter, is the perpetual and visible source and foundation of the unity both of the bishops and of the whole company of the faithful" (*Lumen gentium* 23). This unity is further elaborated when *Lumen gentium* 22 speaks of the authority of the college of bishops. The college has no authority unless united with the Roman pontiff, Peter's successor and its head, but, together with him, it is said to be the subject of supreme and full authority (*subiectum supremae ac plenae potestatis*) over the whole church. Moreover, the office of binding and loosing which was given to Peter (Matthew 16) was also given to the college of the apostles united to its head (Matthew 18). Both of these points had been acknowledged by Bishop Zinelli for the theological commission at Vatican I, but were not placed into the text of *Pastor aeternus*. The concern of some bishops that these statements compromised the full primatial prerogatives of the pope led to several additions to the draft text of *Lumen gentium* 22 in order to strengthen the assertion that the supreme authority of the college is conditioned by its unity with pope.[8] Moreover, the *Nota explicativa praevia* was appended to *Lumen gentium* to further clarify this point and

---

[8] These additions are briefly summarized by K. Schatz, *Papal Primacy: From Its Origins to the Present* (Collegeville, Minn.: Liturgical Press, 1996), 169–70.

to emphasize the pope's freedom in exercising his authority as primate. What do these developments contribute to understanding the relation between primacy and episcopacy?

Consequences for the Relation between the Pope and the Bishops

First of all, those views from the tradition which placed the episcopacy in radical dependence on the primacy, in such a way that all of the authority of the bishops flowed from that of the pope as from its source, seem to have been rejected. Both the sacramental origin of the offices of teaching, sanctifying, and governing as well as the divine institution of the episcopal college count against such views. Thus, on this point, Vatican II did not accept in full the opinions of such eminent theologians as Aquinas, Torquemada, Bellarmine, and Suárez.

Second, the framing of the relation between primacy and episcopacy in terms of the distinction between order and jurisdiction seems to have been, to some extent, superseded. The distinction between order and jurisdiction does not, as such, appear explicitly in the texts of Vatican II. It is implicit in the relatively few times in which the council uses the word "jurisdiction."[9] To the extent that the order-jurisdiction dis-

---

[9] The word *iurisdictio* appears only nine times in the texts of Vatican II (as compared to seven times in the very short text of *Pastor aeternus* of Vatican I)! Of these nine, four concern the relation of exempt religious communities to the jurisdiction of the bishops (*Lumen gentium* 45 and *Christus Dominus* 35 [3 times]), two concern the jurisdiction within the Eastern Catholic churches (*Orientalium ecclesiarum* 4 and 7), one reserves the use of some liturgical books and vestments to those who hold certain types of jurisdiction (*Sacrosanctum concilium* 130), one requires that recent papal teaching about jurisdiction must be interpreted in light of Vatican II (*Nota explicativa praevia* 2), and one states that individual bishops do not enjoy jurisdiction over the universal church (*Lumen gentium* 23). This all suggests that the language of jurisdiction did not play much of a role in the council's thinking about the episcopacy. Even the Code of Canon Law has, by and large, moved away from this language;

tinction concerned the ability to "exercise" episcopal ministry, it would appear that the expression "hierarchical communion" has taken its place.[10] This shift from "jurisdiction" to "hierarchical communion" should not be underestimated. While some have noted that the latter phrase seems to simply juxtapose two differing ecclesiological emphases,[11] nevertheless the very word "communion" could open up a more adequate and reciprocal understanding of the conditionedness of the exercise of episcopal ministry in a way that is not possible within the language of jurisdiction and which, moreover, find roots in the communio-understanding of the church from the first millennium.

Third, the explicit attribution of full and supreme power to the college of bishops brings into sharp focus once again the question of how many subjects of such authority there are in the church. There seem to be only three possible responses to this question: (1) there is one subject of supreme

---

in the entire code the term appears only five times. Canon 29 states that what had been known formerly under the expression "power of jurisdiction" is called now in the Code of 1983 the *potestas regendi*.

[10] The *Nota explicativa praevia*, 2, is especially clear in indicating that the phrase "hierarchical communion" intends to express the fact that "a canonical or juridical determination through hierarchical authority is required for such [ontological] power ordered to action." Here the theological commission introduces a distinction between *munus* and *potestas*, the latter being ordered to action. These distinctions and their implications for the ecclesiology of Vatican II have been carefully analyzed in G. Ghirlanda, *Hierarchia communio: Significato della formula nella "Lumen Gentium"* (Rome: Editrice Pont. Univ. Gregoriana, 1980).

[11] W. Kasper writes: "*Communio hierarchica* is therefore a typical compromise formulation, which points to a juxtaposition of sacramental *communio* ecclesiology and juristic unity ecclesiology. The compromise proved useful at the council, since it made it possible for the minority to agree to the Constitution on the Church. But just to say this is not entirely satisfactory. . . . The synthesis brought about by the last council was highly superficial . . ." (*Theology & Church* [New York: Crossroad, 1989], 158). See also Ratzinger, "La collegialità episcopale dal punto di vista teologico," 754, who calls the expression foreign to the terminology of the ancient church.

authority, the pope, from whom all other authority flows;
(2) there are two subjects, inadequately distinct—the pope
alone and the pope together with the college of bishops; and
(3) there is one subject, the college of bishops, but the pope
may exercise the supreme authority of the college freely, as he
deems appropriate, in virtue of his role as its head.[12] The first
would seem to be excluded by the council's insistence on the
divine institution of the episcopal college and of its authority.
The second may be said to suffer from the weakness of sub-
ordinating the college so much to the pope that it effectively
marginalizes the college as subject of supreme authority.[13]
The third does not seem to preserve sufficiently the personal
nature of the primacy as proposed by Vatican I.[14] Wide-
ranging agreement by theologians about how the subject or
subjects of full and supreme authority are to be understood
and related obviously has not yet been achieved. Yet the very
debate about this issue shows that Catholic doctrine has pro-
gressed to a new perspective for considering the notion of

---

[12] On these possibilities and their relative strengths and weaknesses,
see Y. Congar, "Sinodo episcopale, primato e collegialità episcopale," in
his *Ministeri e comunione ecclesiale* (Bologna: Edizioni Dehoniane, 1973),
161–94.

[13] This theory of two subjects, inadequately distinct, of supreme authority—the pope by himself and the pope together with the college—would
seem to be the view adopted in the *Nota explicativa praevia* 3. Such a view
was dominant among Catholic theologians between Trent and Vatican II
and was defended at the time of the council in W. Bertrams, *The Papacy,
the Episcopacy and Collegiality* (Westminster: Newman Press, 1964).
Antón writes that the *Nota*'s presentation of two subjects could be interpreted in a way that would not easily avoid the danger of marginalizing
the second subject when not actually united with the first (*Il misterio de
la Iglesia*, 2:1025). For this reason he urges that the value of reciprocity,
along with other values such as co-responsibility, representativity, and a
democratic spirit, be characteristic of the exercise of the papacy today.

[14] The view that the college is the one subject of supreme authority was
proposed by K. Rahner, in K. Rahner and J. Ratzinger, *Episkopat und
Primat* (Freiburg: Herder, 1961), 86–93. Y. Congar presents the criticism
of Rahner's view, made by Bertrams and others, in Congar, "Il problema
ecclesiologico del papato dopo il Vaticano II," 154–56.

plenitudo potestas, introduced so long ago toward the beginning of the first millennium.

A fourth point concerns the relation between the individual bishop and the primate. *Lumen gentium* 22 states: "One is constituted a member of the episcopal body in virtue of sacramental consecration and by hierarchical communion with the head and members of the college." That one's membership in the college is based not only upon hierarchical communion but also upon sacramental consecration seems to provide the basis for the statements in *Lumen gentium* 27 that the bishop in his diocese is a vicar and legate of Christ, that he personally exercises a power of governing in the name of Christ which is ordinary and immediate, and that he should not be regarded as a vicar of the Roman pontiff.

> . . . for they exercise the power which they possess in their own right and are called in the truest sense of the term prelates of the people whom they govern. Consequently their authority, far from being damaged by the supreme and universal power, is much rather defended, upheld and strengthened by it, since the Holy Spirit preserves unfailingly that form of government which was set up by Christ the Lord in the Church. (*Lumen gentium* 27)

Here, on the basis of the sacramental foundation of the episcopacy, Vatican II is able to explain more reasonably what Vatican I had merely asserted.

Fifth, the period after the council saw the establishment or reinforcement of a number of institutional structures that expressed the collegial nature of the episcopacy. Of particular note are the general synods of bishops and the national or regional episcopal conferences. The synods are clear expressions of the way in which the relation between primacy and episcopacy can be one of collaboration. The pastoral "apostolic exhortations" that result from these synods are papal teachings addressed to the whole church which have been informed by the contributions of bishops from throughout the world. As "intermediate" structures, the episcopal conferences are quite different and pose a new

question about the relation between primacy and episcopacy. What is the relation between the primacy and an individual episcopal conference? Put another way, what is the
relevance of the collegial episcopal guidance of the church in
a particular nation or region to the wider communion which
includes the whole church? Does the wider community have
a stake in what is decided by national or regional episcopal
conferences? If so, then the primacy, to the extent that it has
a special concern for the well-being of the broader communion, would seem to need to have some relation with the
episcopal conferences.

The Extraordinary Synod of Bishops of 1985, celebrating
the twentieth anniversary of the close of Vatican II, initiated
a new round of discussions by theologians and bishops
about the nature and function of episcopal conferences. One
of the fruits of this dialogue has been Pope John Paul II's
motu proprio on the theological and juridical nature of episcopal conferences, *Apostolos suos (AS)*.[15] The text concerns
less the relation between primacy and episcopacy than the
nature of the college of bishops and the relation of the individual bishop to the episcopal conference, to the college of
bishops as a whole, and to the universal church. A truly fresh
emphasis appears in the idea that, while the individual
bishop cannot "exercise the supreme power which belongs
to the Roman pontiff and to the college of bishops as elements proper to the universal church" (*AS* 10), nevertheless,
the "individual bishops in their ordinary pastoral ministry
are related to the universal church" (*AS* 11). Their careful
guidance of the local church, in the footsteps of Christ the
prophet, priest, and shepherd, already contributes greatly to
the welfare of the whole. Shared pastoral service with other
bishops, expressive of the collegial spirit that unites them,
also promotes the good of the church beyond the particular
diocese of each (*AS* 12). These points tend to underscore the
basic continuity between that service which the bishops per-

---

[15] English translation in *Origins* 28 (1998–99): 152–58.

form when, as the entire college together with the bishop of Rome, they exercise the supreme authority of the church, on the one hand, and that ordinary episcopal ministry exercised individually or in collaboration with neighboring bishops, on the other. The very nature of the ministry of oversight, rooted in the New Testament concept of *episkopē*, is such that it should favor not tension or opposition between primacy and episcopacy but rather their harmonious mutual support.

Vatican II opened many avenues for new forms of ministerial collaboration and invited discussion about the function of and relation between local, regional, and universal structures of authority in the church. After a millennium of emphasizing the unity of the universal church, special recognition was given to the ecclesial reality of the local churches, thus providing a foundation for positively appreciating the pluriformity that rightly comes into being when the proclamation of the gospel encounters the treasures of the many different cultures. It falls in a special way to the college of bishops to live out the tensions of holding together the universal and the particular. The primacy of the bishop of Rome, where Peter witnessed, was given to the church by Christ for the purpose of strengthening the bonds of communion that unite the bishops to one another within the college. The successor of Peter must "strengthen his brothers" (Luke 22:32) in such a way that the proper balance between the one and the many, the universal and the local can be maintained.

Obviously the relation between the universal and the local, and its implications for the relation between the successor of Peter and the other bishops, needs to find practical and institutional expression. Steps such as synods and episcopal conferences have already been mentioned above as positive examples of the reception of the council's initiatives concerning the proper relation between the pope and the bishops. Are other steps possible? One of the more innovative ideas concerning the exercise of the primacy, which has been echoed with approval by several authors, is that of reflecting on the traditional role of the patriarch or regional primate.[16] How does it differ from a primatial ministry that serves the catholic unity of the church as a whole? Could the kind of regional primacy canonized by canon 6 of the very first ecumenical council possibly contribute something valuable today to reflection about and exercise of pastoral ministry in a way that maintains the balance of the one and the many, a balance that surely God wills the community to maintain?

Another topic that could have important implications for our theme is the distinction between the powers of order and jurisdiction. This distinction was often decisive for the way in which the relation between primacy and episcopacy was understood and lived out. Fierce controversies raged about whether or not the pope was the source of all jurisdiction in the church. When Vatican I finally defined papal primacy in 1870, it was understood precisely as primacy of jurisdiction. What is one to make of the fact that jurisdiction plays so little a role in the ecclesiology of Vatican II? Does a juridical vision of the church tend to obscure the vital, sacramental mystery of the church as *koinōnia,* as icon of the Trinity? Of

---

[16] See J. Ratzinger, "Primat und Episkopat," in *Das neue Volk Gottes* (Düsseldorf: Patmos, 1969), 141–46; and J. M. R. Tillard, *The Bishop of Rome* (Wilmington, Del.: Michael Glazier, 1983). Already early in the twentieth century P. Batiffol distinguished three zones of the authority of the bishop of Rome as metropolitan, patriarch of the West, and universal primate (see chapter 3 n. 13 above). Recently the suggestions of two books published by Crossroad Publishing Co. in the Ut Unum Sint series on the primacy offer similar suggestions. H. J. Pottmeyer, in *Towards a Papacy in Communion: Perspectives from Vatican Councils I and II* (1998), 132–35, explicitly proposes the "triadic form of Church structure" (particular church with its bishop and regional ecclesiastical units such as patriarchates and universal church) as providing a necessary foundation upon which the primacy–episcopacy relation can be suitably worked out for today. Michael Buckley's interesting distinction, in *Papal Primacy and the Episcopate: Towards a Relational Understanding* (1998), 62–74, between habitual and substitutional functions of the primatial ministry is yet another concrete suggestion that merits further exploration.

course, it would be presumptuous to assume that a language and practice that had served the orderly exercise of ministry within the community for nearly a millennium does not express a very important aspect of the reality of the community. Therefore, an important area for ongoing postconciliar reflection would seem to be to examine the ecclesial values served by the order-jurisdiction distinction and, perhaps with the help of our Orthodox brothers and sisters or of our other ecumenical partners, to explore how these values continue to be preserved and if there are other ways of preserving them.

At all events, the ecclesiology of communion should help to remove the exercise of authority from the context of struggling over power. When one reads the claims and counterclaims to supreme authority on the part of popes and their opponents, it is difficult for a Catholic not to feel somewhat ill at ease when recalling the gospel passages in which Jesus corrects the apostles for wanting to be the greatest (Luke 22:24–27; Matt. 20:25–28; Mark 10:42–45; John 13:3–16). There is good reason to hope that Vatican II will allow the evangelical perspective of authority as service to frame the way the ministries of primacy and episcopacy are understood and exercised today.

Concluding Reflections

"But I Am among You as One Who Serves."
(Luke 22:27)

In the nineteenth century and well into the twentieth it was quite common for theologians to distinguish between the teaching church (*ecclesia docens*) and the learning church (*ecclesia discens*). When one comes to the end of a short overview of the history of the Christian community—necessarily inadequate even when restricted to one specific theme such as the relation between the ministries of primacy and episcopacy—one is struck by the fact that even the *ecclesia docens*, perhaps especially the *ecclesia docens*, was also very much *discens*. The story of the church is a story of learning, a fact that is not so lamentable when one recalls Paul's beautiful description of ecclesial life under the guidance of its God-provided ministry as a path of growth toward the fullness of maturity in Christ (cf. Eph. 4:11–13). Nor when one recalls that the Master himself, into whose likeness Christians hope to mature, once said: "Learn from me, for I am meek and humble of heart" (Matt. 11:29).

What has the church learned about the primacy and the episcopacy over the course of so many experiences in so many centuries? First of all, it seems evident that history, theology, and official teaching about the relation between the episcopacy and the primacy are intimately related to one another and condition each other. The actual exercise of the primatial ministry of the bishop of Rome in relation to the

158

ministry of the other bishops has taken a variety of forms. Theological explanations have varied substantially, as one can easily verify by recalling the diverse approaches and conclusions that separate such disparate writers as Ignatius of Antioch and Gregory the Great, Torquemada and Febronius, Robert Bellarmine and Cyprian of Carthage. Official doctrine, especially that of the ecumenical councils, has been more modest. Indeed, church teaching has never embraced the more ambitious claims of the theologians. What has it embraced?

Church teaching, especially that of the Catholic Church during the second millennium, has affirmed the divine origin both of the primacy and of the episcopacy, rejecting any radical opposition between the two. It has asserted that the college of bishops needs a head to serve as principle of unity and of coordination. It has taught that the primacy is rooted in the personal promise to Peter and to his successors so that they might serve the collective unity of the episcopacy and of the whole church. It has proposed as necessary to such personal primacy the freedom to effectively foster the unity of the church as a whole, in such a way that this freedom is not legally conditioned by the approval of the episcopacy. It has affirmed that the primacy is bound to respect and collaborate with the episcopacy, which also is divinely established by Christ for the well-being of the church. It has taught that both the college of bishops, as a whole together with their head, and the primate, as head, have an obligation and right to care for the unity of the church as a whole. It has affirmed the sacramentality of the episcopacy and thereby the dignity of each individual bishop as a vicar of Christ in such a way that the primacy does not and cannot diminish that dignity. It has proposed that the primacy and the episcopacy are bound together by ties of hierarchical communion.

It has not explained precisely how these all of these principles function together nor the range of diversity possible in the actual exercise of the relation between primacy and episcopacy. Nor is it likely that it can do so, at least in any definitive way. It is heartening to note that most of the individual points mentioned in the preceding paragraph can also be found in the reflections about the ministry of primacy offered by the Congregation for the Doctrine of the Faith in late 1998.[1] These reflections further suggest that the concrete exercise of the primacy and, therefore, also the concrete integration of those values which the church has discovered over the centuries as governing the relation between primacy and episcopacy must be left open to the needs of the community in any particular stage of its life. What is said of the primacy in general should apply to the particular question of the relation between the bishop of Rome and the other bishops as well:

> The concrete contents of its exercise distinguish the Petrine ministry insofar as they faithfully express the application of its ultimate purpose (the unity of the church) to the circumstances of time and place. The greater or lesser extent of these concrete contents will depend in every age on the *necessitas ecclesiae*. The Holy Spirit helps the church to recognize this necessity, and the Roman pontiff, by listening to the Spirit's voice in the churches, looks for the answer and offers it when and how he considers it appropriate. (§12)

If this is so, then a certain openness to the needs of the times should characterize the relation between primatial and episcopal ministry as well. The basic principles that have been learned over the centuries must be preserved and must guide the way. But their application may take various forms according to the signs of the times. There is a certain freedom of the children of God here, like that which Pope John XXIII is said to have voiced when, as yet apostolic delegate in Paris, on looking over Congar's recently published book on reform, he mused: "Reform of the Church—could it really be possible?"

---

[1] These can be found under the title "Reflections on the Primacy of Peter," in *Origins* 28 (1998–99): 560–63.

Without wishing to minimize the greatness of the attempt of individual believers to follow the gospel values to the best of their ability in any age, one still can hardly avoid finding the earliest part of the story we have considered in this book to be the most inspiring part. The efforts of such heroes as Ignatius or Clement to maintain contact with other churches, encouraging each other and even correcting each other, bears witness to a marvelous sense for the truth that all Christians are united throughout the whole world, forming together the one Body of Christ. The marvelous letters of Cyprian and Gregory the Great show that evangelical respect for each and every local church and for each and every bishop must always be a distinguishing characteristic of the exercise of the Petrine ministry which serves the unity of the whole. When Irenaeus speaks of the succession of bishops to the apostles and when Leo writes of the unique succession of the bishop of Rome to Peter, unmistakable is their conviction that these ministries come from Jesus himself. Their proper exercise is a matter of faithful discipleship to him.

In a special way, two of Leo's contributions to the council of Chalcedon, which at first might seem a bit arrogant, may perhaps, on further consideration, prove particularly instructive. Regarding the christological doctrine to be defined, Leo insisted that the council fathers not come up with any teaching other than that contained in his letter to Flavian. Regarding canon 28, Leo insisted that a new order in the church could not be mandated by the change of the capital of the empire. Was he just serving himself in these positions, exalting his own teaching and defending his own higher rank above the other bishops? I think not. Regarding doctrine, he was afraid that a new conciliar discussion could result in a repetition of the disastrous decision to support a heresy, which had just happened two years earlier at the infamous "robber synod" of Ephesus (449). His insistence that the teaching in his letter to Flavian be accepted was not based on the fact that he personally wanted to be acknowledged as the absolute doctrinal authority within the church. Rather he insisted on his letter because the letter was true; it faithfully taught the truth about Christ. No vote could alter that fact. Thus, his stance about the doctrine of Chalcedon was rooted in his defense of the primacy, not of himself, but of the truth about Christ.

I believe that something similar can be said about Leo's view of canon 28. The actual "ranking" of churches is not nearly so important as the reason given to justify ecclesial order in the first place. Leo saw canon 28 as embracing the principle that primatial structure within the church is ultimately based on nothing more than pragmatic or political considerations. If that be the case, then primacy would have no solid theological foundation. His insistence on the Petrine roots of primacy is not a claim for his own primacy, but once again for the primacy of Christ. Christ is the head of his church. It must be in Christ, in his relation with the disciples as made known to us through the Word of God, that the foundations of the primatial ministry are to be found.

The two conciliar documents that, up to the present time, history has bequeathed to us with the name "Constitution on the Church" both begin in a way that gives pause for reflection. In contrast to a secular constitution, even a rather good one like that of the United States of America, which opens with the words "We the people," *Pastor aeternus* of Vatican I and *Lumen gentium* of Vatican II both begin with expressions that are names for Jesus Christ. Jesus is the "eternal shepherd"; Jesus is the "light of the world." This happy circumstance (or was it circumstance?) contains a hidden wisdom. All authority, all structure and order within the church must take its cue not from any secular models of government, as good and praiseworthy as they may be, but from some other source. Church order in some profound way partakes of and expresses the mystery of communion which flows out from the reality of God. For this reason believers guided by the Spirit, like Francis of Assisi, to give but one example, tend to treasure authority as a gift. Should it be seen in that way, surely we are justified in being confident that authority will be exercised by all, both by those who are charged with the task of oversight (*episkopē*) and by the one who must allow Peter's unique service of unity to live on, in the spirit of him who said: "Whoever among you wishes to be first (*prōtos*) shall be the servant (*doulos*) of all" (Mark 10:44).

Index

Acacian Schism, 84–90
Acacius, 84, 85
Alberigo, G., 113n. 26, 126n. 16,
    130n. 2, 131n. 4, 134n. 10, 135n.
    12, 136n. 13
Ambrose, 67, 80–83
Anastasius of Thessalonica, 73–74,
    100, 104
Anciaux, P. 109n. 17
Anicetus, 29, 40, 66
Antón, Angel, 13n. 7, 88n. 9, 107,
    109nn. 16, 18; 112n. 24, 117,
    118nn. 2, 3; 119nn. 5, 6; 124n.
    13, 133n. 8, 134n. 10, 135n. 11,
    142n. 32, 143n. 1, 145n. 4, 152n.
    13
apostolic succession, 24; papal pri-
    macy and, 31n. 2
Arius, 17, 53, 55
Arles, Council of, 52
Athanasius, 56–57, 58, 66, 82
Athenagoras (patriarch), 101
Augustine, 64
Augustinus Triumphus, 111, 126

Ballerini, P., 135
baptism, 44, 45
Bardy, G., 41n. 14
Basel-Ferrera-Florence-Rome, Council
    of, 122–23
Basilides (bishop), 42–43
Basil the Great, St., 44, 82
Batiffol, Pierre, 46n. 16, 62n. 13, 63n.
    13, 64n. 15, 82n. 38, 156n. 16
Bauer, Walter, 16, 17,
Beinert, W., 21n. 9
Bertrams, W., 152n. 13
Betti, U., 138n. 19
Bévenot, M., 47, 48

bishop(s), 9, 20, 24; apostolic succes-
    sion and, 24; authority of, 59; col-
    lege of, 29, 134–35, 136, 146–49;
    as foundation of local church, 27;
    conferences of, 153–54; relation
    of, to pope, 11, 95, 132, 150–57;
    relations among, 27, 29; role of,
    131–36; selection of, 105–9; and
    structure of Christian community,
    25n. 14; synods of, 153. *See also*
    collegiality; episcopacy; pope
bishop of Rome: appeal to, 63; prima-
    tial role of, 58. *See also* pope; pri-
    macy
Bolgeni, G. V., 135–36
Boniface, 65, 95, 97
Boniface VIII (pope), 117; *Unam
    sanctam,* 117–18
Bossuet, J.-B., 132
Boulgakov, S., 137
Brandenburg, A., 19
Brown, Raymond E., 8, 20nn. 6, 7;
    30n. 1, 31n. 2
Buckley, Michael, 156n. 16

Cajetan, 123, 129
Camelot, P.-Th., 68n. 18
cardinals, 113–16; college of, 113–14,
    131. *See also* collegiality
Carrasco, A., 110n. 19
Carthage, Council of, 49, 63
Caspar, E., 105n. 7
Celestine (pope), 65, 67, 68, 69, 70,
    83
Celestius, 63, 64
Chalcedon, Council of, 65, 75–80, 83,
    85, 90, 91, 109, 110n. 18, 161
Charlemagne, 87, 95, 97

Christian community: structure of, 22, 24–25; unity of, 21, 130
Christianopulo, E. D., 135
church order, 45; before Council of Nicaea, 15–29
Cipriani, S., 19n. 6
Clement of Rome, 7, 20–25, 29, 36, 161; *Letter to the Corinthians,* 7, 30, 32, 39
clergy, 10n. 8. *See also* presbyters
collegiality, episcopal, 113–14, 127, 130–31. *See also* bishop(s); cardinals
Colombo, C., 137n. 16
conciliarism, 116, 117–28, 141
Congar, Yves, 10n. 4, 12n. 7, 83n. 40, 98n. 26, 102n. 1, 103n. 3, 104n. 4, 105nn. 6, 8; 107, 109n. 18, 111nn. 21–23; 114n. 27, 115n. 29, 117, 118n. 2, 119n. 6, 121n. 9, 123n. 11, 134n. 10, 136n. 14, 140nn. 28, 29, 30; 144, 145n. 4, 152nn. 12, 14; 160
Constance, Council of, 119–22, 131, 132; *Haec sancta,* 120–21
Constantine, 51–59, 66, 80; Donation of, 95
Constantinople: as capital, 55, 60; First Council of, 39, 55, 58, 59, 78, 83, 89, 91; Fourth Council of, 79, 99–101; Second Council of, 77, 85, 89, 90, 91; Third Council of, 85, 93
Conte, P., 93n. 21
Corecco, E., 110n. 19
Cornelius (bishop of Rome), 41, 43, 46
Council of the 318. *See* Nicaea, Council of
councils, 113–16; ecumenical, 28, 58, 120, 135
Counter-Reformation, 129
Coxe, A. Cleveland, 35n. 8
Cyprian of Carthage, 11, 25–29, 41–44, 45–50, 56, 59, 71, 73, 135, 159, 161
Cyril of Alexandria, 67, 68, 82; twelve anathemas of, 85

Damasus (pope), 57, 58, 60, 61, 62n. 13, 65, 66, 67, 74, 81n. 37, 82n. 38, 89
Deferrari, Roy J., 47
Dejaifve, G., 12n. 7, 112, 119n. 4,

127n. 17, 133n. 7, 134n. 10, 137nn. 15, 16; 141n. 30
De Maistre, J., 136
de Margerie, B., 129n. 1
Dewan, W. F., 137n. 16
Diocletian, 17, 52, 66
Dionysius (bishop of Corinth), 31, 34
Dionysius of Alexandria, 34
Dioscorus (bishop of Alexandria), 76, 77
Docetists, 23n. 11
Domnus of Antioch, 76–77
Donation of Constantine, 95
donatism, 52–53
Donatus, 52
Donfried, Karl P., 20n. 6
Dupuis, J., 117n. 1
Dvornik, F., 60, 99n. 28

edict of Milan, 51
edict of toleration, 52, 80
Eleuterius, 35
Eno, Robert, 23n. 11, 25n. 14, 27, 31n. 2, 34, 35n. 8, 39n. 12, 61, 70n. 22, 82, 82n. 39, 90n. 12
Ephesus, Council of, 65, 68, 69–70, 76, 83, 91
episcopacy: necessity of, 27; offices of, 145, 150; relation of, to primacy, 80, 105, 111, 113–16, 134, 138, 143, 150–57, 158–63; sacramentality of, 144–50
episcopalism, 132
Eucharist, 28; and ministerial structure of church, 20–21
Eugene IV (pope), 122
Eusebius of Caesarea, 11, 15–17, 39, 39n. 12, 50, 51, 52, 80
Eusebius of Nicomedia, 55, 56
Eutyches of Constantinople, 75–76, 82, 85
excommunication: bishops and, 28
Extraordinary Synod of Bishops of 1985, 154

Farmer, William R., 32, 37, 38n. 10
Febronianism, 132, 134–35
Febronius (J. N. Hontheim), 133, 134n. 9, 159
Firmilian (bishop of Caesarea), 44, 45
Flavian (bishop of Constantinople) 75–77, 82, 161

Florence, Council of, 124–26; *Laeten-tur caeli,* 124
Fourth Lateran Council. *See* Lateran
Frend, W. H. C., 85n. 2
friars, 113–16
Fuellenbach, J., 30n. 1
Fuhrmann, Horst, 94n. 22

Gallican Articles, 132–33
Gallicanism, 106n. 9, 132–35, 138n. 17, 141–42
Gelasius I (pope), 84–90
Gerbert, M., 134–35
Germanus (patriarch of Constantinople), 96
Gerson, John, 119–20, 132
Ghirlanda, G., 151n. 10
Giles of Rome: and papal hierocracy, 117
Gratian (emperor), 61, 110, 115n. 29
Gregorian reform, 102–16, 117, 128
Gregory II (pope), 95, 98
Gregory VII (pope), 102–16, 133; *Dictatus Papae,* 105–6
Gregory XII, 121
Gregory of Nazianzus, 58
Gregory the Great (pope), 10, 84–101, 103, 159, 161

Hamer, J., 137n. 16
Hamill, Patrick, 16n. 2
Harnack, Adolf, 33, 34
Hartmann, G., 98n. 26
Henn, W., 17n. 4
Hennesey, J., 109n. 15
Henoticon, 85, 88
Hertling, Ludwig, 8n. 2, 29n. 19
Hiereia, Council of, 96–97
Hilary, 62, 67
Himerius of Tarragona, 61
Holstein, H., 125n. 15
Honorius I (pope), 93, 100
Hontheim, J. N. *See* Febronius
Hormisdas (pope), 84–90; Formula of, 89, 100
Horn, Stefan, 80nn. 35, 36
Humbert of Silva Candida (cardinal), 101, 103

Ibas of Edessa, 76–77, 89
iconoclasm, 96
Ignatius (patriarch), 99
Ignatius of Antioch, 9, 10, 20–25, 27, 28, 29, 32–33, 34, 36, 159, 161

Innocent I (pope), 57n. 5, 61, 63, 64, 65, 67, 82
Innocent III (pope), 79, 111
International Theological Commission, 9n. 3, 25n. 14
Irenaeus of Lyon, 11, 20–25, 29, 32–33, 34, 35–36, 37, 40, 59, 113, 161

James of Viterbo: and papal hierocracy, 117–18
Jerusalem "Council," 19
Jimenez-Urresti, T. I., 138n. 21
John VIII (bishop of Rome), 101
John XXIII (anti-pope), 120
John XXIII (pope), 143–44
John Chrysostom, 66, 67, 83
John Paul II (pope), 13, 154; *Apostolos suos,* 154–55; *Ut unum sint,* 13
Josephism, 132
Juan of Torquemada, 112, 123, 129, 150, 159
Judaizers, 23n. 11
Julius I (bishop of Rome), 56, 66
jurisdiction, power of, 109–13, 130, 146
Justin I (emperor), 88
Justinian (emperor), 63n. 13, 84, 89

Kasper, W., 137n. 16, 142n. 32, 151n. 11
Kereszty, Roch, 32n. 4, 36n. 9, 41n. 13
Kirch, C., 54n. 3, 81n. 37

lapsed, the, 41–43
Lateran: Fifth Council of, 123; Fourth Council of, 41, 42–43, 44, 56, 59, 71, 73
law: primacy and, 107–8
Lécuyer, J., 83n. 40, 144n. 3, 145n. 4
Leo III (pope), 87, 96
Leo IX (pope), 101
Leo the Great (pope), 11, 57, 62, 65, 66, 70–79, 83, 84, 85, 90, 91, 93, 104, 161–62
letters: between bishops, 29; circular, 8; as reflection of life of apostolic churches, 7; role of, in Christian community, 7; as source of information about bishops, 11
Liberius (bishop of Rome), 57
Linus (bishop), 36
Lucentius, 77

Lucius, 42
Lyon: Second Council of, 108n. 13, 125–26

Maccarrone, M., 104n. 4
Macdonald, J., 74n. 27
Marchetto, A., 98n. 26
Marcian (emperor), 43, 44, 76, 78
Marot, H., 31n. 3
Marsilio of Padua, 119
Martial (bishop), 42
Martimort, A. G., 132n. 5
Martin I (pope), 93
martyria (witness), 24
Maxentius, 51
Maximus the Confessor, 93
McCue, James, 22n. 10, 27n. 16, 31n. 2
Meier, John, 30n. 1
Melchers, Bishop, 138
mendicant orders. *See* friars
Michael (emperor), 99
Michael Cerularius (patriarch), 101
Michael Paeleologus, 125
Milevius, synod of, 63n. 14
Miltiades, 52
Minnerath, Roland, 27n. 16, 29n. 20, 38n. 11, 137n. 17, 140nn. 28, 29
Mirbt, Carl, 68n. 17
Moeller, C., 122n. 10
monepiscopacy, 31; papal primacy and, 31n. 2
monophysites, 85, 89, 92, 94
monothelitism, 92–94
Murphy, F. X., 77n. 30

Natalis (bishop), 92
Nero, 35
Nestorianism, 75–76
Nestorius, 67, 68, 69, 85, 89
Neuner, J., 117n. 1
Newman, Cardinal, 68
Nicaea: First Council of, 10, 11–12, 17, 28, 29, 50, 53–58, 62, 78, 81, 86, 91; creed of, 66, 85; Second Council of, 96–97
Nicene controversy, 57
Nicephorus (patriarch), 97
Nicholas I (bishop of Rome), 99
Nicholas of Cusa, 122
Novatian (anti-pope), 41

O'Collins, G., 18n. 5
O'Grady, John F., 18n. 5

Origen, 26–27
order, power of, 109–13, 130
ordination, 145; absolute, 109–10; episcopal, 28, 146

papal states, 95
Paul VI (pope) 101
Paul of Samosata, 50, 66
Pelagian controversy, 63
Pelagius, 63, 64
Pelagius I (pope), 90
Pelagius II (pope), 90
Peri, V., 97n. 24, 98n. 27
persecution, 52
Pesch, R., 20n. 6
Peter Damian, 103
Peter Mongos (patriarch of Alexandria), 85, 86
Peter of Ailly, 119–20, 132
Peter of Alexandria (bishop), 81
Philips, G., 148n. 7
Photius (patriarch), 99–100
Piepkorn, Arthur C., 58n. 6, 60n. 8, 62n. 13, 63n. 13, 69n. 21
Pistoia, Synod of, 134
Pius VI (pope), 134, 136
Pius IX (pope), 141
plenitudo potestatis (fullness of power), 104, 119–21, 122, 124–25, 153
Polycarp of Smyrna, 23n. 11, 29, 40, 66
Polycrates of Ephesus, 39–40
pope: local churches and, 113, 139; relation of, to bishops, 11, 12, 18, 132, 150–57; as successor to Peter, 136; word, 9. *See also* bishop(s); bishop of Rome; episcopacy; primacy
Pottmeyer, H. J., 137n. 16, 156n. 16
presbyter, 9, 20; and structure of Christian community, 25n. 14
presbyteroi (appointed elders), 19, 20n. 8
primacy, 18, 87, 136; of bishop of Rome, 26–27, 30–31; exercise of, 29; of jurisdiction, 33; law and, 107–8; meaning of, 29; of ordinary power, 79; Petrine justification of, 59–65; relation of, to episcopacy, 80, 95, 105, 111, 113–16, 134, 138, 143, 150–57, 158—63
primatial leadership, 39–45

Proterius (bishop of Alexandria), 77
Pseudo-Isidore, 133; Decretals, 11, 98, 106n. 9, 115n. 29
Puglisi, James, 127n. 17
Pulcheria (emperor), 76

Quasten, Johannes, 16n. 2, 33, 34, 34n. 5, 82n. 38
Quinisext Synod, 54

Rahner, Karl, 152n. 14
Ratzinger, Joseph, 10, 27, 50, 109n. 16, 142n. 32, 145n. 4, 146n. 6, 151n. 11, 152n. 14, 156n. 16
Reformers, Protestant, 126, 129
Reumann, John, 20n. 6
Richer, E., 132, 134n. 9
Rimini, Council of, 57
Rivière, J., 104n. 5
Robert Bellarmine, 129–30, 150, 159
Rome: bishop of, 44; church of, 31; relation of, to eastern churches, 62n. 13, 65–70
Rufus (bishop), 65
Ryan, J. J., 110n. 19

Sardica, Council of, 11–12, 56–57, 62, 82, 86, 87
Schatz, Klaus, 12n. 7, 66, 87n. 7, 93n. 18, 96n. 23, 102, 103n. 2, 106n. 11, 121n. 8, 124n. 12, 132n. 6, 149n. 8
Schwartz, E., 68n. 19
Sergius (patriarch of Constantinople), 93
Simplicius (pope), 85
Siricius, 61, 63, 65, 82
Soter (bishop of Rome), 31
Staniforth, Maxwell, 1n. 1, 20n. 8
Stephen (bishop of Rome), 42–45, 47, 49
Suárez, Francisco, 130–31, 150
"successor to Peter" (title), 26, 38–39
Sullivan, F. A., 24n. 13
Sylvester (pope), 95
Symmachus (pope), 87
synods, 28

Tamburini, Pietro, 134
Tertullian, 37, 38, 45
Theodore of Mopsuestia, 89
Theodoret of Cyr, 76, 77, 82, 89

Theodosius I (emperor), 58, 81
Theodosius II (emperor), 57, 75, 76
Theophilus, 67
Thiel, A., 86nn. 4, 6; 88n. 8
Thils, G., 138n. 17
Thomas Aquinas, 110–12, 145, 150
Thomas of Vio, 123
Tierney, B., 12n. 7, 108n. 14, 114n. 28
Tillard, J. M. R., 156n. 16
Timothy Aelurus (bishop), 77
Torquemada. *See* Juan of Torquemada
Torrell, J. P., 137n. 16
Trajan (emperor), 20
Trent, Council of, 123–28, 131, 145n. 4, 152n. 13; Counter-Reformation and, 129

Ultramontanism, 136
Unger, Dominic, 36n. 9
unity: supralocal, 28–29
Urban, H. J., 19n. 6

Vacca, S., 86n. 5
Vatican Council I, 12, 92, 94, 115n. 29, 116, 128, 136, 137–42; *Pastor aeternus,* 92, 138–40, 141n. 30, 142n. 31, 147–49, 162; primacy and, 35n. 8; primacy of jurisdiction and, 33; teaching of, about relation of pope and bishop, 12
Vatican Council II, 12, 107, 116, 130, 143–57; *Lumen gentium,* 146–49, 153, 162; teaching of, about relation of pope and bishop, 12
Vicentius of Capua, 57
"vicar of Christ" (title), 86, 104
Victor of Rome, 29, 39, 40, 45, 66
Vigilius (pope), 89, 90
Vogel, Cyril, 28, 28n. 18, 55
von Döllinger, Johann J. Ignaz, 115n. 29

Western Schism, 115, 117–28
William of Ockham, 119
Wolter, H., 125n. 15

Zachary (pope), 84, 94–95
Zeno (emperor), 85
Zosimus (pope), 57n. 5, 61, 62, 64, 65, 74